DAVID
ADJAYE
FORM
HEFT
MATERIAL

DAVID ADJAYE

FORM

HEFT

MATERIAL

Edited by Okwui Enwezor and Zoë Ryan, in consultation with Peter Allison

With essays by David Adjaye, Peter Allison, Okwui Enwezor, Andrea Phillips, Zoë Ryan, and Mabel O. Wilson

With a foreword by Douglas Druick and Okwui Enwezor

The Art Institute of Chicago and Haus der Kunst, Munich

Distributed by Yale University Press, New Haven and London

Dedicated to the memory of Stuart Hall

David Adjaye: Form, Heft, Material is published in conjunction with an exhibition organized by the Art Institute of Chicago and Haus der Kunst, Munich.

Haus der Kunst, Munich
January 30–June 28, 2015

The Art Institute of Chicago
September 19, 2015–January 3, 2016

The exhibition catalogue *David Adjaye: Form, Heft, Material* has been underwritten by Nancy C. and A. Steven Crown.

Major funding for the exhibition at the Art Institute of Chicago has been generously provided by Nancy C. and A. Steven Crown and Barbara Bluhm-Kaul and Don Kaul.

The Auxiliary Board of the Art Institute of Chicago is the Lead Affiliate Sponsor.

Allstate is a Supporting Corporate Sponsor.

Additional support for the exhibition has been provided by the Fellows and Benefactors of the Architecture and Design Department, the Architecture & Design Society, Cheryl and Eric McKissack, the Graham Foundation for Advanced Studies in the Fine Arts, and Linda Johnson Rice.

Further support for this exhibition has been provided by Knoll.

Knoll

Annual support for Art Institute exhibitions is provided by the Exhibitions Trust: Kenneth Griffin, Robert M. and Diane v. S. Levy, Thomas and Margot Pritzker, and the Earl and Brenda Shapiro Foundation.

First edition
Printed in Belgium

Cataloging-in-Publication Data is available from the Library of Congress
ISBN 978-0-300-20775-0

Published by
The Art Institute of Chicago
111 South Michigan Avenue
Chicago, Illinois 60603-6404
www.artic.edu

Distributed by
Yale University Press
302 Temple Street
P.O. Box 209040
New Haven, Connecticut 06520-9040
www.yalebooks.com/art

Produced by the Department of Publishing of the Art Institute of Chicago

Sarah E. Guernsey, Executive Director
Edited by Amy R. Peltz
Production by Joseph Mohan
Photography research by Lauren Makholm
Proofreading by Hilary B. Becker

Book design by Mode, London
www.mode-online.co.uk

Separations, printing, and binding by Die Keure, Bruges

Cover design: Latticework pattern by Adjaye Associates, adapted from the facade of the National Museum of African American History and Culture, Washington, D.C. Graphic design by Mode, London.

CONTENTS

The exhibition catalogue *David Adjaye: Form, Heft, Material*
has been underwritten by Nancy C. and A. Steven Crown

Major funding for the exhibition at the Art Institute of Chicago has been generously provided by Nancy C. and A. Steven Crown and Barbara Bluhm-Kaul and Don Kaul.

The Auxiliary Board of the Art Institute of Chicago is the Lead Affiliate Sponsor.

Allstate is a Supporting Corporate Sponsor.

Additional support for the exhibition has been provided by the Fellows and Benefactors of the Architecture and Design Department, the Architecture & Design Society, Cheryl and Eric McKissack, the Graham Foundation for Advanced Studies in the Fine Arts, and Linda Johnson Rice.

Further support for the exhibition has been provided by Knoll.

Knoll

Annual support for Art Institute exhibitions is provided by the Exhibitions Trust: Kenneth Griffin, Robert M. and Diane v. S. Levy, Thomas and Margot Pritzker, and the Earl and Brenda Shapiro Foundation.

DIRECTORS' FOREWORD
DOUGLAS DRUICK &
OKWUI ENWEZOR

David Adjaye stands at a pivotal point in his career. With an ever-expanding portfolio of civic architecture, public buildings, and urban planning commissions stretching from Europe to the United States, Africa to Asia, and Russia to the Middle East, he has garnered a laudatory critical response, and his stature as an architect, teacher, and thinker continues to grow. Over the past two decades, beginning with his first office (Adjaye and Russell, formed in 1994) and now at the eponymous Adjaye Associates, established in 2000, his practice has evolved from the design of critically praised domestic buildings to award-winning public, municipal, and social structures.

An important hallmark of Adjaye's architecture is his transformation of complex ideas and concepts into legible and approachable structures that address their contexts and urban environments. Just as his work responds to different locales with varying building traditions and legacies of modernism, it also engages the complex geographical, ecological, technological, engineering, economic, and cultural systems that shape the practice of architecture globally. Many of Adjaye's commissions have been built in contexts where the intersection of cultural diversity, histories of migration, transitions in social formations, and changes in urban processes have created dynamic cosmopolitan centers. These contexts have called for envisioning architecture that is rooted in the neighborhood and community but is also dynamic, experiential, and innovative. The rigorous attitude that has shaped Adjaye's thinking makes him one of the leading figures in the generation of architects under fifty years of age whose practices reflect the changing landscape of global architecture.

Haus der Kunst and the Art Institute of Chicago are pleased to have collaborated on this substantial presentation of Adjaye's work. This survey exhibition, the largest and most expansive of its kind to date, constitutes an important milestone, as it permits an in-depth examination of the most significant projects of the last fifteen years. Along with the exhibition, the accompanying catalogue, *David Adjaye: Form, Heft, Material*, explores the core architectural and design principles that impart legibility and distinctiveness to Adjaye's work. Through the choreographic and narrative dispositions of the buildings and a series of recurring ideas and motifs, the lineaments of his critical thinking and experimentation emerge. These are encapsulated in how elaborated and pared-down forms combine to give iconographic shape to his structures, whether they are a small pavilion for a playground in the East End of London; an art pavilion built of hand-finished timber on the Croatian coast; an academic campus on the outskirts of Moscow; a monumental national museum in Washington, D.C.; or public housing in Harlem, New York. The diversity of location and function of these projects attests to Adjaye's broad-based practice. But it is in the buildings themselves, especially their craft and use of materials, that his critical vision is most evident. The buildings' heft not only gives the structures a sculptural solidity, it elucidates and defines their physical presence, thus enlivening the experiential particularities of the materials and their responses to ecological, geographic, technological, and environmental situations.

Our institutions, and especially the curators of the exhibition—Zoë Ryan, John H. Bryan Chair and Curator in the Department of Architecture and Design at the Art Institute of Chicago, and Okwui Enwezor—express gratitude to the lenders, collaborators, and donors whose generous support has made the project possible. Our heartfelt thanks go to Nancy C. and A. Steven Crown, who have underwritten this exhibition catalogue. On behalf of Haus der Kunst, we acknowledge all members of the Adjaye exhibition committee: Tony and Elham Salame, the Aïshti Foundation; Michael Hue-Williams, Albion Barn; East Deck; Design Indaba; Ford Foundation and Darren Walker; Amalia Dayan and Adam Lindemann; Gaby and Wilhelm Schürmann, Berlin and Herzogenrath; and Jürg Zumtobel, Zumtobel. Further contributions have been provided by Tim Noble and Sue Webster, Lorna Simpson, Mark Falcone, Nicola Ferguson-Lees and Colin Gibbons, and Jonathan Liebmann. We also extend our appreciation of our shareholders—Freistaat Bayern, the Schörgruber Group, and the Gesellschaft der Freunde Haus der Kunst—for their outstanding and continued engagement with, and annual funding support of, Haus der Kunst.

The Art Institute of Chicago acknowledges major funding for the exhibition from Nancy C. and A. Steven Crown and Barbara Bluhm-Kaul and Don Kaul. We are grateful to the Auxiliary Board of the Art Institute of Chicago for its Lead Affiliate Sponsorship and to Allstate for its Supporting Corporate Sponsorship. Additional support for the exhibition has been provided by the Fellows and Benefactors of the Architecture and Design Department, the Architecture & Design Society, Cheryl and Eric McKissack, the Graham Foundation for Advanced Studies in the Fine Arts, and Linda Johnson Rice. Further support for the exhibition has been provided by Knoll. Annual support for Art Institute exhibitions is provided by the Exhibitions Trust: Kenneth Griffin, Robert M. and Diane v. S. Levy, Thomas and Margot Pritzker, and the Earl and Brenda Shapiro Foundation.

This exhibition has been greatly enriched by the generosity of our lenders. Our gratitude goes to Christine Kron at Museum Fünf Kontinente in Munich for lending the two magnificent sculptures by Olowe of Ise, which inspired the soon-to-be iconic tiered design of the Corona of the National Museum of African American History and Culture in Washington, D.C. Additionally we acknowledge the Aïshti Foundation; Michael Hue-Williams, Albion Barn; Karen Brusch, Gallery Momo; Knoll, Inc.; and the Moscow School of Management Skolkovo for lending key works. For their support in the production of models and architectural fragments for the exhibition, the Art Institute of Chicago and Haus der Kunst also acknowledge Mark Falcone, Wilhelm Pfalzer & Hans Vogt GmbH & Co. KG, VHB Memmingen, and Architectural Polymers, Inc.

A special mention goes to everyone at Adjaye Associates. From the inception of the project, the members of this team have ensured that all the needs of the exhibition were met, and they were essential to helping our institutions navigate the complex network at the center of Adjaye's practice. Without their contributions, the exhibition would not have been possible.

Finally, we wish to express our thanks to David Adjaye for entrusting his work to us and sharing his ideas and passion for architecture with us. We hope this exhibition deepens the public's understanding of his buildings, the rigor of his vision, and the pertinence of the cultural and historical influences that inform them. Our respect and admiration for his accomplishments over the last fifteen years are equaled only by our anticipation of those yet to come.

ACKNOWLEDGMENTS
OKWUI ENWEZOR
& ZOË RYAN

This exhibition and catalogue have been realized thanks to a wide network of visionary and talented people to whom we are greatly indebted. First, and most importantly, we give special thanks to David, with whom we have engaged in a sustained dialogue since 2011. We are immensely grateful to him for his enthusiasm, engagement, and incredible generosity during our numcrous visits to his offices. These discussions were enlivened by site visits to many buildings in London; Lagos, Nigeria; New York; Denver, Colorado; Washington, D.C.; and Beirut, Lebanon, among others.

Our immense gratitude and thanks go to the exceptionally talented team at Adjaye Associates, in the London, New York, Berlin, and Accra offices, including Ashley Shaw Scott Adjaye, Ama Ofeibea Amponsah, Yohannes Bereket, Woonghee Cho, Mitesh Dabasia, Mansour El-Khawad, Joshua Ellman, Andreina Feijoo-Gomez, Chris-Marit Gieseke, Sulaiman Hakemy, Emilia Izquierdo, Tanji Kaler, Jessica King, Gayle Markovitz, Michael Matey, Asako Mogi, Eleonora Pedoni, Matthew Rauch, Eleni Sofroniou, and Paul Tse. Their collaborative spirit, generosity, and unfailing creativity were essential to this project. Without their dedication, knowledge, and efficiency, the exhibition would not have been possible. The exhibition has further benefited from the commitment and knowledge of Peter Allison. As David's teacher and longtime collaborator, as well as the author and editor of several monographs on his work, Peter has provided immeasurable critical insight while serving as curatorial and editorial consultant. We also thank the authors of the essays—Andrea Phillips, Mabel O. Wilson, and Peter—for their insightful analyses of key facets of Adjaye's practice. Sincere appreciation also goes to Mode, especially Phil Costin, Darrell Gibbons, and Lluis Camps, for creating this beautifully designed book.

The Art Institute of Chicago and Haus der Kunst, in collaboration with Adjaye Associates, commissioned a documentary film, *Collaboration(s): A Portrait of the Architect through the Eyes of Others*, that explores David's work through the viewpoints of artists, clients, critics, curators, and essayists whose collaborations and engagements with him and his practice provide further insights into his architecture. We especially thank the director of the film, Oliver Hardt, as well as Peter Adjaye, Peter Allison, Olafur Eliasson, Thelma Golden, Julie Mehretu, Chris Ofili, Taiye Selasi, Lorna Simpson, Deyan Sudjic, and Sue Webster. The essays and film provide a variety of perspectives and ways of understanding the different ideas presented in the exhibition.

At Haus der Kunst, adjunct assistant curator Anna Schneider has been an exceptional and integral member of the project, overseeing and coordinating every aspect of the exhibition within the museum and serving as principal liaison between all of the partners. Other members of the staff who have ensured that the project meets the highest standards include: Marco Graf von Matuschka; Teresa Lengl, Iris Ludwig, and Dr. Sonja Teine; Ulrich Wilmes; Isabella Kredler; Andrea Saul; Elena Heitsch; Anna Schueller; Martina Fischer; Tina Anjou; Jacqueline Falk; Chris Gonnawein and Funny Paper; Christian Gries and Kulturkonsorten; Tina Kohler, assisted by Sofia Nilsson; Cassandre Schmid; and Anton Kottl, assisted by Glenn Rossiter.

At the Art Institute of Chicago, special thanks go to the members of the outstanding team in the Department of Architecture and Design: Alison Fisher; Karen Kice; Lori Boyer; Jennifer Breckner; Daniel Dorough; Gibran Villalobos; Alicja Zelazko; and the department's volunteers and interns, Ariane Cherry, Mia Khimm, Kathryn Loeb, and Temple Shipley. We would also like to acknowledge members of the Department of Publishing for their exceptional work on this catalogue and the exhibition, in particular, Sarah Guernsey, Amy Peltz, Joseph Mohan, Lauren Makholm, Wilson McBee, and former colleague Robert Sharp. Appreciation goes to our Department of Imaging, headed by Louis Meluso, with Christopher Gallagher and P. D. Young. We would like to express our thanks to Jeffrey Wonderland and his talented team in the Department of Graphics. We also acknowledge Gordon Montgomery and Erin Hogan for their insights and help in promoting this exhibition.

The Department of Museum Registration under Jennifer Draffen—in particular, Darrell Green and Jennifer Oberhauser—was invaluable in executing the transportation of exhibition items. Sara Urizar and exhibition designer Yau-mu Huang provided expert advice and assistance during the installation, as well as its planning. We acknowledge the legal staff of the museum, in particular, Julie E. Getzels and Maria Simon. In addition, many thanks are due to our Department of Development, led by Eve Coffee Jeffers, especially Stephanie Henderson, George Martin, Jennifer A. Moran, Jennifer Oatess, and Jamie Summers. We express our gratitude to current and former members of our conservation staff—Antoinette Owen, Kimberly J. Nichols, Kristi Dahm, Emily Heye, Suzanne Schnepp, Christine Fabian, Sylvie Penichon, Lauren Chang, and Isaac Facio—for their careful attention to each exhibition object. In the Department of Physical Plant, we are most thankful to William Caddick and Thomas Barnes as well as foremen Joseph Vatinno, George Yovkovich, Anthony Nakvosas, and their staff for their commitment to this exhibition. We also thank John Molini, Michael Kaysen, Michael Hodgetts, Craig Cox, and all of the shipping and installation staff for their care in handling and presenting the works of art. Thanks also go to Raymond Carlson Jr., William Foster, and Tom Riley in the Department of Media Production and Services. In addition, we acknowledge the contributions of Michael Neault and former colleague Carissa Kowalski Dougherty, both from the Department of Digital Experience and Access, and Kevin Lint from the Department of Telecommunications and Network Services. Our gratitude goes to the Department of Protection Services, especially Russell Collett, Thomas Henkey, Margie Skimina, and Salvatore Seminara.

In the Department of Museum Exhibitions we thank Megan Rader and former colleague Dorothy Schroeder. We are also grateful for the work of Jeanne Ladd and Dawn Koster in the Department of Museum Finance. Finally, our heartfelt appreciation goes to Douglas Druick, President and Eloise W. Martin Director, for his belief in this project and continued support throughout, and to both Chief Operating Officer David Thurm and Deputy Director for Art and Research Martha Tedeschi.

We hope that this is just the begining of a lively and sustained cross continental dialogue about the work of David Adjaye.

INTRODUCTION
OKWUI ENWEZOR
& ZOË RYAN

Since gaining early recognition for a series of unique London homes made for a coterie of art world friends from the late 1990s to the mid-2000s, architect David Adjaye has developed an increasingly varied and robust portfolio of distinctive architectural works. He approaches the making of buildings as an artist would, fusing artisanal craft with a highly refined use of unusual materials. This results in structures imbued with the qualities of handcrafted objects, structures with a sculptural heft that belies the complex technical and technological principles by which they were constructed. Adjaye's architecture eschews the empty signifiers of the overproduced designs that currently bedevil much contemporary architecture due to the indiscriminate application of digital mapping. Rather, the hallmarks of Adjaye's architecture are form, heft, and material. His thinking is, however, by no means constrained by this vocabulary. His engagement with the physical presence of architecture acts as a generator and a combustion node for broader intentions: from shape to thought, from material to experiment, from structure to landscape. His buildings are not based on delivering a singular style. Each structure and space is treated from the point of view of its unique architectural context and geolocational memory.

Adjaye's earliest projects include houses at both ends of the economic spectrum. But he has also designed public buildings—including libraries, museums, markets, civic centers, and cultural institutions—that deal directly with logics of secular and civic commemoration. This aspect of his practice, which has involved creating architecture that responds to the checkered histories of voluntary and involuntary migration, has offered occasions for exploring how neighborhoods evolve and change, how new communities are created, and how diverse urban identities and experiences are woven into the tapestry of multicultural difference. More recently, his practice has grown to tackle complex, large-scale urban forms via the development of master plans for urban areas and for cultural and educational campuses. His work now takes him across the world, with endeavors in Europe, Asia, Africa, and North America. Yet his approach remains consistent. Both personal and particular, it is driven by an insatiable desire to continually improve the built landscape and generate projects that teach us about the world in which we live.

Born in Dar es Salaam, Tanzania, in 1966, to Ghanaian parents who were diplomats, Adjaye spent his early life in Africa and the Middle East, and his formative years in Egypt, Lebanon, Yemen, and Saudi Arabia. His family relocated to the United Kingdom in 1979. With offices in London, New York, Berlin, and Accra, he is currently itinerant, like many global architects whose practices defy cultural borders and geopolitical categories. Such practitioners travel constantly as part of a generation of "suitcase architects" (to borrow a term from theorist Ken Tadashi Oshima) who fluidly cross social and political boundaries in a form of architectural shuttle diplomacy.[01] Adjaye is, however, unique in being an African-born architect working in a global landscape. He moves among his offices and the far-flung sites to which his work is bringing a distinctive contemporary "Afropolitan" view.

01.   Ken Tadashi Oshima, "Spatialities of Suitcase Architects," in *Travel, Space, Architecture*, ed. Jilly Traganou and Miodrag Mitrasinovic (Ashgate Publishing, 2009), pp. 254–55.

Adjaye's education at Southbank University and then the Royal College of Art honed his creative process. Graduating with a master's degree in architecture in 1993 in the United Kingdom, which had experienced over a decade of political and social upheaval, he found an affinity with a generation of artists whose work explores social issues and provides alternative perspectives on daily life. Among these friends are Chris Ofili, Tim Noble, and Sue Webster, with whom Adjaye has worked closely on projects ranging from homes and studios to exhibition designs. Speaking of his time at the Royal College of Art, Adjaye notes, "For two years I was immersed with artists. And that's when my relationship to art and using art as a way to understand the contemporary became very fertile for me."[02]

Since opening his first studio in 1994 with William Russell in the East End of London, and then in 2000 starting his own practice (now seventy people strong, across four offices), Adjaye has avoided adhering to a single style. Indeed, his early buildings seem to constitute discrete statements. Now, however, with close to fifty built projects, the majority of which are cultural institutions, it is possible to decipher the codes of practice to which Adjaye has hewed, and to understand more clearly how each of his ideas has developed out of and advanced the preceding one. Often working in cities struggling with diversity and difference, his public buildings—especially the libraries and cultural centers—provide spaces that foster links among people and marry the creative industries with entrepreneurial endeavors.

In fact, Adjaye's trajectory has never been haphazard but rather carefully orchestrated, with one project building on the next as a way to cultivate his methodology and approach and demonstrate his potential for tackling diverse, ever-more complex commissions. For example, the mix of white-walled galleries and studios coupled with living spaces in his initial house designs positioned him as an adroit and sensitive creator of art spaces, able to translate the needs of artists into architecture, which paved the way for the larger-scale museum commissions that followed—Rivington Place in London and the Museum of Contemporary Art Denver in Denver, Colorado, both completed in 2007—as well as proposals that were shortlisted, such as those for the New Museum in New York and the San Francisco Museum of Modern Art.

Committed to a cosmopolitan approach to architecture, Adjaye struggled as a student with the narrow focus of architectural education. As he recalls, "the schools only taught from the canon of the West. It was very difficult to look beyond it, to other references. And nobody ever wanted to talk about what was different, only about what was similar to European architecture. They wanted to see me as different, but they didn't want my architecture to be different."[03] While in school, Adjaye visited buildings in Europe and Japan. Since then he has continued to engage in theoretical research coupled with on-the-ground observation. Between 2002 and 2006, Adjaye hosted a series of BBC television and radio programs for which he traveled to countries such as Brazil and India to undertake interviews with architects including Charles Correa and the late Oscar Niemeyer. Adjaye thus made his own studies a public affair, while also becoming a spokesperson for architecture from beyond the Western canon.[04]

02.   David Adjaye, in conversation with Zoë Ryan, Feb. 19, 2013.

03.   Jeff Chu, "Luminous: David Adjaye," *Fast Company*, Sept. 10, 2009, www.fastcompany.com/design/2009/featured-story-david-adjaye.

04.   Horst Rutsch, "Trying to Look at Architecture Differently," *UN Chronicle* 43, 2 (July–Aug. 2006), p. 45.

Considering research and writing essential aspects of his practice, Adjaye could be described as a consummate student. He energetically travels the globe to experience the work of other architects firsthand, furthering his understanding of the field so that he may develop designs that transcend these earlier examples. In particular, he has studied the work of modern architects— yet he is not bound by their conventions. Rather he reinterprets them with influences drawn from other traditions, both Western and non-Western, particularly African abstraction. These insights help him find appropriate responses to the climate, lifestyles, and visual and material sensibilities of each project's site, thus generating outcomes that are both his own and embedded in a sense of place.

In 2011 Adjaye published the multivolume work African Metropolitan Architecture, a compendium of photographs he had taken over a period of more than ten years while traveling to every capital city (with the exception of Mogadishu) in all of the continent's then fifty-three sovereign states. This effort to understand Africa and its contribution to world architecture has proven essential to Adjaye's subsequent efforts to develop projects there. The research has differentiated his practice and allowed him to advance his agenda of promoting a global definition of architecture, one that is committed to "engagement with the world."[05] As he insists, his work is "not about my own intimate scenarios but about architecture in an expanded field."[06] This directive also aligns him with architects such as Aldo Rossi, who believed that "'personal expression' matters very little or not at all, unless it has a place in society and a place in history."[07] Now working on projects across continents and on a variety of scales ranging from pavilions and private residences to public buildings and entire urban corridors, Adjaye has continued to develop a tool kit of methods and techniques for everything from how he makes spaces to what materials he chooses. This tool kit expresses his desire to rethink conventions, replacing them with designs that speak to the specific time and place in which they were created. These ideas are made especially manifest in important recent projects, such as the National Museum of African American History and Culture (NMAAHC) in Washington, D.C., a building that faces history head on by bringing together visual references from across Africa and America to create a design that is both visually and physically evocative.

Not meant to be absolute or engineered to seal his legacy, the present publication, which accompanies an exhibition organized by Haus der Kunst and the Art Institute of Chicago and presented in spring and fall 2015, respectively, captures a significant moment in Adjaye's vibrant practice. Zoë Ryan's essay provides an overview of the architect's career to date, charting the path from his early studies and first houses to his public buildings and urban systems, making the case that by "rooting his projects in place, memory, and material qualities, he uses architecture as a platform to reexamine entrenched social rules and modes of human behavior." David Adjaye tells a personal account of his eleven-year research project in Africa and the influence of its findings on his subsequent methods and approaches. Okwui Enwezor discusses Adjaye's designs for the NMAAHC and the Cape Coast Slavery Museum in Cape Coast, Ghana, analyzing how they serve as ad hoc monuments to the African experience in the Black Atlantic in order to address aporias of

05.   Ibid.

06.   Ibid.

07.   Aldo Rossi, "Three Projects," in Aldo Rossi: Buildings and Projects, ed. Peter Arnell and Ted Bickford (Rizzoli, 1985), p. 10.

memory and history while engaging discourses of social agency and diasporic imagination. Andrea Phillips focuses on Adjaye's public buildings in the United Kingdom, such as the Idea Stores and the Bernie Grant Arts Centre, all in London, and demonstrates how their success derives from their negotiation of the landscape of these complex urban areas, encouraging, through their informal qualities, the asking of questions about spatial and social equity. Peter Allison traces how Adjaye builds on existing design concepts in his work. Taking us through a careful examination of typologies such as "cityspace," defining "frontages," and enclosing "open spaces," Allison posits that Adjaye has developed a set of strategies that he has constructively applied throughout his projects as a means of enlarging the scale and scope of his practice. Finally, Mabel O. Wilson concentrates on the NMAAHC, calling attention to the new style Adjaye has deployed for it, which acknowledges black contributions to American history but also challenges assumptions about national identity and race through a detailed analysis of the founding mission of its umbrella organization, the Smithsonian Institution. Between the essays appear portfolios of Adjaye's architecture and design projects, each focusing on a different theme or area of his practice. Accompanied by brief introductions from Peter Allison, these surveys further illuminate the evolution of Adjaye's work. Read together, these new interpretations of his output provide insights into a robust career and promote a deeper understanding of an architect who aims to create projects of profound social and cultural significance and meaning.

Note to readers: Throughout the book, the titles of works by David Adjaye are underlined in the text and fully capitalized in captions.

"ARCHITECTURE IS ABOUT
WHERE WE ARE, HOW WE ARE,
AND WHERE WE WANT TO GO."
DAVID ADJAYE

WAYS OF BUILDING
ZOË RYAN

(Fig 01) SEVEN
New York, 2004-10
Exterior view showing adjacent
schist foundations

Ways of Building
Zoë Ryan

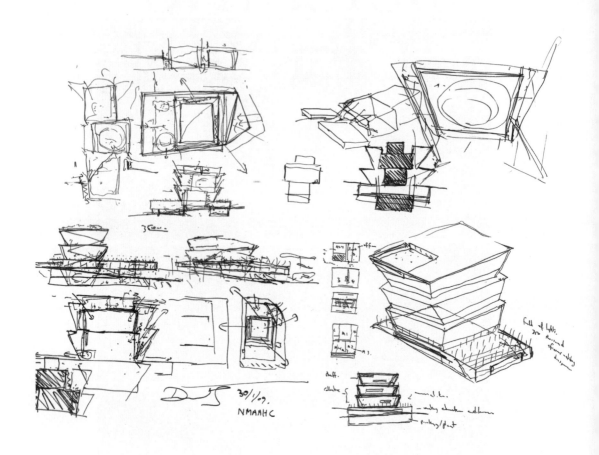

(Fig 02) NATIONAL MUSEUM OF
AFRICAN AMERICAN HISTORY AND CULTURE
Washington, D.C., 2009-16
Design studies

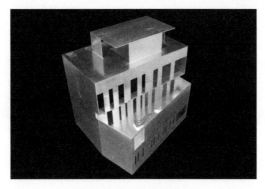

(Fig 03) SILVERLIGHT
London, 2002-09
Rear facade, model

David Adjaye is an unconventional thinker. Deeply connected to the arts and culture, he is committed to exploring the social implications of buildings and has spent the last fifteen years generating forms of architecture that convey his ideas about the world and exemplify his open, explorative, and layered approach. Rooting his projects in place, memory, and material qualities, he uses architecture as a platform to reexamine entrenched social rules and modes of behavior. Now appearing across Europe, Africa, Asia, Russia, and the United States, Adjaye's buildings not only provide new readings of historical motifs and architectural typologies but are also imbued with significance and meaning that connects them with their varied contexts.

Through a range of methods—careful sequencing of space, thoughtful material choices, sensitive selection of color palettes, and attention to the relationship between inside and outside—Adjaye makes his buildings, whether public or private, large or small, insist on being accommodated as objects that share the space with those who inhabit them. From his early houses and larger public structures in London, to subsequent international projects, he has demonstrated a sustained commitment to creating buildings that address larger cultural and social implications, are responsive to place, prompt user engagement and investigation, and question the role of architecture in shaping our relationship with the world around us.

Adjaye has developed a toolbox of methods and approaches through which he tests his ideas. Although rooted in modernism, his work is not bound by its conventions. Rather than perfecting the eloquent studies of structure and function initiated by architects in the first part of the twentieth century, he unapologetically plays with modernism's clean lines and essential forms to better understand their inherent logic, using them as a model to create new typologies. Although inspired by how his predecessors addressed societal change, he is well aware of modernism's failure to generate the ambitious outcomes to which it aspired, as well as the commercialization of its ideals in many of the buildings that have since come to define international skylines. Adjaye eschews modern architecture's drive for singular outcomes and one-fits-all solutions and instead develops approaches more mindful of the unique characteristics of a place (such as its climate, geography, and culture) and of contemporary conditions. "The modern project created templates but not solutions," he has noted. "I borrow from the efficiencies and intelligence of modern architecture—how it translated the industrial world to the architecture world and thought about density and the articulation of horizontal and vertical planning. I use this as a framework."[01] His reinterpretation of modernist practices draws influences from Western and non-Western traditions. Adjaye's ultimate aim is to make spaces that respond to their context and allow for inhabitation and appropriation, while providing a frame for understanding and experiencing the world around us.

The title of this essay is inspired by John Berger, who wrote, "We only see what we look at. To look is an act of choice." See John Berger, *Ways of Seeing* (1972; repr., Penguin Books, 1990), p. 8.

01. David Adjaye, in conversation with the author, July 18, 2013.

METHODS & APPROACHES

Like works of art such as paintings and sculptures, Adjaye's buildings require users to enter into a relationship with them, to reconcile their own preconceptions and prior experiences of architecture with the carefully controlled and framed conversation with which they are currently confronted. Even the names that he gave his first house commissions (Elektra House, Dirty House, Sunken House, and Lost House, all in London) resemble titles artists would assign works of art. Evocative yet full of ambiguity, they suggest narratives and incite individual readings. This inventive approach may stem from Adjaye's art school education. While a graduate student at the Royal College of Art (RCA), he came to know many of the artists with whom he has enjoyed long-lasting collaborations, including Chris Ofili, Tim Noble, and Sue Webster. Here too he formed a concern for creating buildings that tell us about the time and place in which we live. The conceptual phase of his designs continues to be defined by strategies he developed at the RCA—research (regarding both the content and aesthetics of projects), hands-on making of models, and loyalty to sketching and drawing—rather than by the digital methods that are now more conventional.

Adjaye begins every project with a series of sketches, many of which are penned early in the morning when he can find time alone to think about an idea and make it visible on paper. Inspired by site visits, conversations with clients, and other on-the-ground research, his drawings possess an energy and spontaneity that suggest the character of a place as much as they articulate a formal response. Arrows denoting entrances and connections to the urban frame; halos of dashes (the language of cartoons) marking the areas that will be flooded with natural light; and hastily written texts stipulating materials, structural elements, public areas, and so on, provide clues to the relationships Adjaye envisions between his projects and their inhabitation and use. His sketches should not, however, be read in the tradition of artist's preparatory sketches for paintings and sculpture. They depict complete ideas and, although they may be light on detail, it is uncanny how many of the finished designs look exactly like these original thoughts. (Fig 02)

Once he has developed his sketches to a point where he feels he has achieved a "synthesis, a moment of originality" with a design that transcends what he and others have done before, Adjaye begins to work with his team.[02] Together they flesh out the design, testing its merits until they have a concept that can be fully realized. In the past ten years, as computer software has evolved, Adjaye Associates has increasingly used digitally sketched-up volumes to test scale and proportion in context, as well as other aspects of projects. Yet even when employing digital technologies, handmade marks remain at play, and the team employs physical models to craft solutions that might not be discoverable by computer. The first rudimentary models, constructed from foam or cardboard, add physicality to the form and give "a sense of the presence of a building."[03] A quick succession of handmade models are then crafted by members of the studio at a range of scales to decide on the geometries of the design, assess its proportions, develop construction methods, and determine its ultimate material composition. (Fig 03) These are often developed into seductive presentation models using materials as diverse as bronze, wood, and laminated cardboard. The team will commission 1:1 scale mock-ups of parts of buildings for up-close scrutiny early on to ensure the details are correct. Through a process of iterative experimentation and refinement, Adjaye's hands-on approach results in projects that combine functional imperatives with creative expression and that test new formal solutions, material applications, and contextual relationships.

02.   Adjaye, in conversation with the author, Feb. 19, 2013.

03.   Ibid.

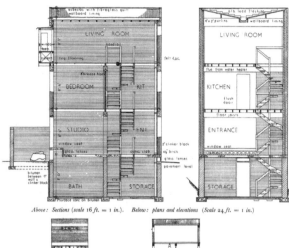

Above: Sections (scale 16 ft. = 1 in.).   Below: plans and elevations (Scale 24 ft. = 1 in.).

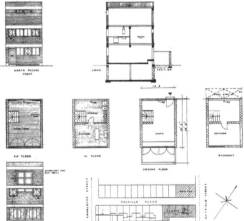

HOUSE IN SOHO, LONDON

Alison and Peter Smithson

' The attempt was made to build in Central London, and failed because of difficulty with adjoining owners. It seemed that a series of Trusts held the surrounding land (all bombed) but it turned out to be one man who intended to build kitchens to the left, W.C.'s to the right and restaurants to the rear—this contract was about to be signed after nine months' work.

On the normal city site costing between 15s. and 25s. per sq. ft. one can apparently do little different from the Georgian, but it was considered that a different internal order must be visualised. The air and sunlight of the attics in the daytime suggests that living quarters should be up top, with the bathroom in the cool of the dim basement.

It was decided to have no finishes at all internally—the building being a combination of shelter and environment.

Bare concrete, brickwork and wood. The difficulty of unceiled rooms was satisfactorily overcome by the disposition of rooms which were also placed high up or low down according to light-sunlight desired.

Brickwork may suggest a blue or double burnt or coloured pointing; but the arbitrary use of colour and texture was not conformed with, and common bricks with struck joints were intended. The bars and colour variation have some sort of natural tension when laid by a good bricklayer.

In fact, had this been built it would have been the first exponent of the " new brutalism " in England, as the preamble to the specification shows : " *It is our intention in this building to have the structure exposed entirely, without internal finishes wherever practicable. The Contractor should aim at a high standard of basic construction as in a small warehouse.*" '   **P.D.S.**

Erratum : The four houses shown above were inadver-tently incorrectly listed in the contents on the front cover of last month's issue of " A.D."

342

(Fig 04) Alison and Peter Smithson,
"House in Soho, London," *Architectural Design*
(December 1953), p. 342.

MAKING SPACE

Adjaye's first significant body of work was a series of houses and studios for artists and other creatives built in London from the late 1990s to the mid-2000s. With these projects he investigated ideas and identified areas of interest, establishing the basis for his subsequent, more complex explorations at a larger scale. Later preoccupations—experimenting with materials; using color and light to direct circulation, space, and overall composition; the context of buildings and how this can afford opportunities for examination of cultural and creative values—play out provocatively in these London houses.

Adjaye's home designs are distinguished from his public buildings by their interiority. Rather than continually reminding users of the connection between the inside and outside of the building, his private projects are peppered with occasional moments of heightened awareness of these relationships, while maintaining an overwhelming sense of being enclosed. He achieves this through a highly choreographed articulation of space. Windows are used sparingly, to frame views and create moments of pause. The structures often open up in the back or at the top to views of the city and sometimes lack street-facing windows. This protects the privacy of the inhabitants, as well as recalling caves or tombs: the timeless basic conditions of a shelter—a recurring theme. For buildings with a public mission, however, Adjaye employs an altogether different strategy to encourage users to interact with the structures. Formal devices such as prow-like corners and cutbacks in the facade at street level make clear the buildings' roles as civic institutions that welcome the public.

In all Adjaye's projects, he emphasizes the journey through the building by carefully orchestrating the space. This is felt most pointedly in his houses. He places walls and stairs and employs materials, light, and color to create interconnected but differentiated spatial experiences within a single structure. Built-in furniture, as well as freestanding furniture elements that relate to the interior architecture, help define spaces: the cabinets and raised platforms in the bedrooms of Silverlight in London, and the custom bathrooms and rooftop terraces of LN House in Denver, Colorado, for example. These furniture elements, seamlessly embedded in the visual language of the whole project, are also useful—a modernist combination of form and function.

The relationship between the paths inhabitants take within a building and the building's form is a central theme in Adjaye's designs. As Adolf Loos did in his Raumplan houses, Adjaye directs movement through the use of sequential layouts and additive configurations of networks of spaces, stacked one above another.[04] The networks respond to the underlying conditions at each level and often lead to a living space on the top floor (as in Silverlight, Dirty House, and Sunken House, for example). Similar ideas also appear in early-twentieth-century work by practitioners such as Frank Lloyd Wright, whose buildings often unfold from the inside out, establishing integral connections between plan and elevation, interior space and external expression, architecture and decoration. In Adjaye's homes, the narrow circulation spaces that open into light-filled wells and communal areas enhance the choreography of exploration, thrusting users into a close relationship with their surroundings and emphasizing a process of compression and decompression.

The specificity of Adjaye's houses is based on the lives of the clients and an understanding of their needs: "The disconnect between the object and the person needs to be reversed, and replaced by a closer sense of engagement."[05] He has become an adept translator of personal aspirations

04. "Where we spoke of the floor plan hitherto, since Loos we can speak of a space plan." See Heinrich Kulka, *Adolf Loos* (Anton Schroll, 1931), p. 14, quoted in Johan van de Beek, "Adolf Loos: Patterns of Town Houses," in *Raumplan versus Plan Libre: Adolf Loos and Le Corbusier, 1919–1930*, ed. Max Risselada (Rizzoli, 1988), p. 46. Heinrich Kulka was a pupil of Adolf Loos.

05. Ibid., p. 7.

and interests. In <u>Seven</u>, a New York house, he created a series of spaces meant to accommodate works of art ranging from a large-scale painting by Jean-Michel Basquiat to a floating sculpture by Maurizio Cattelan. In <u>Silverlight</u>, which reveals itself only through exploration, a wall on an upstairs level is paneled in recycled tortoiseshell salvaged by its owners, rather than a more conventional material. Downstairs, the cabinets and countertops in the laundry room are finished in recycled plastic. Such touches, which might seem incongruous with the angular geometries and spare aesthetic, imbue the project with personal details, thus ensuring that the building truly reflects the lives of those who inhabit it.

This is not to say Adjaye overlooks the connections between structure and site in his domestic projects. "As found" elements on the site are incorporated in meaningful ways (an idea borrowed from architects Alison and Peter Smithson and discussed below). In <u>Sunken House</u>, the main window in the living room on the second floor frames a view of a large oak tree that provides a natural canopy. In <u>Seven</u>, Adjaye reveals the bedrock and lower sections of a party (or shared) wall at the back of the house, creating a tension between the history of the site and the new concrete structure. (Fig 01) In addition, in an ode to another of Adjaye's heroes, a scattered arrangement of geometric windows on the facade of the building echoes Marcel Breuer's Whitney Museum, located around the corner.

<u>Elektra House</u> in London has the overall proportions of the adjacent Victorian terrace houses, yet its window-free facade, clad with panels of phenolic (resin-coated) plywood, makes it appear "other." The materiality of this house owes much to the influence of the Smithsons and subtly recalls the monolithic structure of their unbuilt Colville Place house, designed in 1952.[06] (Fig 04) In this and subsequent projects, the Smithsons used raw materials such as cast concrete, exposed brick, and untreated timber to demonstrate "the intensity of the direct and unspectacular."[07] Their approach appeals to Adjaye, who also finds inspiration in daily life for creating designs with an authentic relationship to their context. Indeed, many of his ideas— above all his straightforward forms constructed of simple geometries, executed in commonplace materials—find parallels in the work of these late architects, particularly their designs from the 1950s and 1960s, which sought "forms with a certain autonomous, archetypal and vernacular quality."[08] The Smithsons embraced the "as found" concept (itself inspired by Jean Dubuffet and other practitioners of Art Brut) and were particularly interested in engendering "a new seeing of the ordinary, an openness as to how prosaic 'things,' could re-energize our inventive activity."[09] Their influence on Adjaye is most visible in projects such as <u>Seven</u>, with its exposed foundations, and <u>Dirty House</u>, where the site's East End context inspired the design. The rough finish of the anti-graffiti coating on the facade reflects the gritty urban character of this part of London and endows the building with the raw presence of the small workshops that characterize the mixed-use neighborhood. Like the Smithsons, Adjaye avoids pastiche. With an eye on contemporary vernaculars, he focuses on recontextualizing materials to avoid comparison with earlier traditions. The results are often unexpected, as in the facade of <u>Elektra House</u>, but by reinterpreting local architectural motifs and cultural norms, his projects more readily speak to the time in which they were made and shed light on contemporary concerns.

06.   Alison and Peter Smithson, *The Charged Void: Architecture* (Monacelli Press, 2001), pp. 96–97. Earlier in their career, the Smithsons' title for this project was "House in Soho, London."

07.   Claude Lichtenstein and Thomas Schregenberger, eds., *As Found, The Discovery of the Ordinary: British Architecture and Art of the 1950s* (Lars Muller, 2001), p. 13.

08.   Alison Smithson, *Alison and Peter Smithson: From a House of the Future to a House of Today* (010, 2004), p. 19.

09.   David Robbins, ed., *The Independent Group: Postwar Britain and the Aesthetics of Plenty* (MIT Press, 1990), p. 201.

Ways of Building
Zoë Ryan

(Fig 05) IDEA STORE WHITECHAPEL
London, 2001-05
Escalator and suspended lobby

(Fig 06) MUSEUM OF CONTEMPORARY ART DENVER
Denver, Colorado, 2004-07
Exterior view showing corner entrance

GOING PUBLIC

The guiding principles of Adjaye's practice—distinguishing between public and private spaces, internal and external relationships, vernacular and formal languages—are even more evident in his designs for public buildings, which are emphatic in their questioning of notions of institutional space. His first major projects in London attest to his interest in creating public buildings that rethink existing typologies and are explicit about their community function. This is immediately apparent in the composition of their facades and in their internal spaces, which reflect the multiplicity of the urban realm with which they are in conversation. As Adjaye insists, "for me, the architecture of engagement is the public realm. So civic, educational, cultural, faith-based, governmental work is really a rich arena to create the archetypes that change society or move society forward."[10]

The Idea Store program was an ambitious initiative undertaken by the borough of Tower Hamlets in London's East End. Adjaye was responsible for the first two projects to be realized, the Idea Store Whitechapel and the smaller Idea Store Chrisp Street. Reflecting retail sector concepts, the use of the word *store* rather than *library* was intended to encourage access to education, the arts, and culture, thereby increasing consumption of knowledge as opposed to commercial goods. In response, Adjaye literally extended the public realm into the building. At the Idea Store Whitechapel, the glass facade nudges over the pavement like the prow of a ship, interacting with the adjacent street market and inviting people to enter. The front facade stops short of the ground, forming a suspended lobby. Like similar devices in Adjaye's early houses, it cleverly transitions users from the street into the building, simultaneously heightening their awareness of their surroundings. The suspended lobby protects an escalator that also encourages people to move into the building.(Fig 05) Once inside, instead of grand, hushed reading rooms, visitors encounter informal spaces for communal gatherings, more private areas, and studios. Adjaye explains, "When I say a building becomes a public space, [I mean] that the building re-enacts the confidence of the users into feeling that this is a space for them on their own terms."[11]

One critic has said of the Idea Store Whitechapel that it transitions from a colorful, lustrous exterior to a "rough 'packing case'" interior.[12] But this seems to be missing the point. Adjaye has long bemoaned the relegation of materials research to what he calls issues of performance and historically assigned notions of quality. Instead, he seeks to employ materials to produce spaces that resonate with their users and more effectively accomplish their missions. For example, in the Idea Store Whitechapel, Parallam fins soften the internal appearance of the external wall, as well as restrict sun penetration.[13] In addition, plywood furniture and bookshelves make the spaces feel informal and invite use, further emphasizing the inclusive nature of the building. This recalls the work of Louis Kahn who, in projects such as the Philips Exeter Academy Library in Exeter, New Hampshire, designed timber-lined niches "where a person is alone near a window … a kind of discovered place in the folds of construction."[14] In Adjaye's building, the fins also serve an environmental function, diffusing light and sound.

The Idea Store buildings were the first in a series of London public buildings that Adjaye designed. Each involved a recently conceived institution locating itself in a specific environment. In keeping with the aims of the program, both of Adjaye's Idea Stores were close to markets and

10.   Adjaye, in conversation with the author, July 22, 2013.

11.   Ibid.

12.   Roger F. Stephenson, "Word on the Street," *RIBA Journal* 112, 11 (Nov. 2005), p. 14.

13.   Parallam is a product that utilizes recycled timber. Its generic name is "parallel strand lumber" and its strength is greater than the natural species from which it is made.

14.   Louis Kahn quoted in "The Mind of Louis Kahn," *Architectural Forum* 137, 1 (July–Aug. 1972), p. 77.

local shopping centers, and on major traffic arteries, which were considerations in their architecture. The Stephen Lawrence Centre, on the other hand, is situated in a residential area in southeast London, where Stephen Lawrence was murdered in a racist attack at a bus stop in 1993. As a memorial to the eighteen-year-old student, the building celebrates his intention to become an architect, offering short courses to children interested in design and the environment. The structure's tapering volumes express hope and resignation in equal measure.

Rivington Place is home to two arts organizations: Iniva (Institute of International Visual Arts) deals with non-Western art, and Autograph ABP is a picture agency representing black photographers. Situated in a tight-knit area occupied by small businesses and a scattering of bars and restaurants, the building's proportions echo those of older buildings in the vicinity, and the black walls and the expanding window pattern suggest the control of photographic exposure by camera diaphragms, or the use of black paper as a framing material when assessing images. By contrast, the Bernie Grant Arts Centre is an addition to a line of Neoclassical civic buildings standing on one side of a triangular green space in a north London suburb. Bernie Grant was the first black member of Parliament and represented this area. The center encourages local young people to take a professional interest in the performing arts, in which black Britons and other minority communities are underrepresented. Purpleheart, the richly colored timber lining the foyer of the auditorium building, is imported from three countries in South America, including Guyana, where Grant was born.

In short, in his public buildings, Adjaye does not engage with overly abstract architectural theories. Rather, he imbues these projects with history and significance by alluding to local contexts and crafting designs that invite in the public. Not interested in laborious searches for the ever-elusive "new," he embraces salient lessons from the architecture of all periods, juxtaposing them with inventive new ideas that endow his projects with contemporary meaning.

FIRST INTERNATIONAL PROJECTS

Throughout his career, Adjaye has worked at a variety of scales, from exhibition designs and private residences to large public buildings, but the overall trend is toward projects of ever-greater scope and complexity. Adjaye's design for the Museum of Contemporary Art Denver (MCAD), finished in 2007, allowed him to expand his sphere of influence and test his ideas internationally, translating his knowledge of developing institutional spaces to the American context. (Fig 06) Adding a cultural voice to the city's development program, the exterior employs a contemporary international idiom but adapts it to the context and the role of the building. The body of the museum is a reflective gray cube supporting a timber-clad volume at roof level that cantilevers over the adjacent alley to take advantage of this extra space while leaving the street free at ground level.

An informal entranceway—a cut in the corner of the building—leads to a ramp that delivers visitors into the heart of the museum, and from there into a series of spacious galleries and an elegant wood-paneled library. Gone are the grand staircases of nineteenth-century museums; instead, Adjaye places the entrance to the museum on the same level as the street, purposely connecting it to the urban environment. This openness to the city welcomes visitors inside and serves as a physical and visual reminder of the museum's public mission. On the upper floor, the main galleries are enclosed by passage-like spaces with occasional floor-to-ceiling windows that frame views of the city, fusing the micro scale of the museum with the macro scale of the city.[15] Just as Adjaye's earlier projects embrace and extend the city, the interior of MCAD is conceived as a pedestrian-friendly urban environment. The rooftop restaurant and terrace encourage visitors to move through the building and prolong their stay by enjoying these gathering spaces at its pinnacle. This enhances the feeling that this museum is made for public occupation.

Adjaye's next international project, the Moscow School of Management Skolkovo, completed in 2010 on the outskirts of Moscow, also called for the reinvention of a type. (Fig 07) He again grounded the design in the history of modernism—on this occasion, the radical architecture and art of revolutionary Russia. Commissioned as part of President Vladimir Putin and Prime Minister Dmitry Medvedev's vision for a new high-tech park on the southwestern fringes of Moscow, the 460,000-square-foot megastructure, situated on a twenty-seven-acre field, functions as a self-contained campus for the school. Because the site is some distance from the city center, Adjaye aimed to create a building that is hyperdense and multifunctional (especially important in a landscape that is covered in snow eight to nine months of the year). He explains, "Whether it is a tiny project or a large one, the idea of making a microcosm of the city is a great stimulus."[16]

The school was the first building constructed in this new park, and Adjaye created a design that rethinks conventional university campuses. Rather than four buildings surrounding a classical quadrangle, the structure is one interconnected form. The elevated entrance floor (with parking beneath) is a disc that houses the reception area and teaching spaces, as well as a 3,500-seat conference facility. The block- and bar-shaped buildings placed at angles on top of the disc house the administration, leisure facilities, student accommodation, and a hotel. There are obvious references to the work of Russian avant-garde architects such as Konstantin Melnikov and El Lissitzky, whose drawings explored time and space, line and plane, and volume and color. Its massive scale, with 130-foot cantilevered slabs, evokes Lissitzky's Wolkenbügel (literally, "cloud-irons"), skyscrapers topped with horizontal blocks that project out over the ground below, which he proposed for major intersections of the Boulevard Ring in Moscow. (Fig 08)

In addition to its scale and formal structure, the Moscow School of Management Skolkovo is distinguished by the overt use of patterns on its facade. Referencing the lozenge-shaped windows of the Melnikov House in Moscow, the tessellated pattern of the windows develops a visual language that is both inherently local and internationally recognizable. (Fig 09) In a subtle range of colors, bands of leaning shapes suggest folds and ridges in the facade, as well as lateral movement. The distribution of the variously colored panels is intended to enhance the changes in light conditions over the course of a day: the gold panels of the recreational block are illuminated by western light, while the gray and blue panels of the residential wings receive northern and southern light, respectively. Reflecting and refracting light, the panels affect how the building is seen, depending on the time of day and the angle from which it is viewed. They also serve a practical purpose, directing and diffusing light as it enters the building. "The patterned silhouette has the potential to refer to the present whilst suggesting the future," explains Adjaye. This decorative facade both stimulates user engagement and provides a dynamic visual syntax for the building.[17]

15.   Marina Lathouri, "The Intimate Metropolis: Frame and Fragment; Visions for the Modern City," *AA Files*, no. 51 (2005), p. 61.

16.   Adjaye, in conversation with the author, July 22, 2013.

17.   David Adjaye, *Output* (Toto, 2010), p. 9.

ADAPTING TO LOCAL & GLOBAL CONDITIONS

To adequately appreciate Adjaye's increasingly international portfolio, we must recognize how he marries universal creative languages with ideas derived from, or connected with, the context in which they are constructed. As theorist Nikos Papastergiadis has asserted, "the culture of cosmopolitanism … lives within the aesthetic domain of transnational networks and on local streets."[18] Adjaye has become increasingly attentive to location-based imperatives (be they climate, lifestyle, or visual and material sensibilities) yet frames these as part of broader, international dialogues. This has helped position his work in a larger sphere of influence. He remains concerned with making his projects function as urban systems and networked structures with strong identities that can nevertheless accommodate change. Adjaye understands this kind of change as depending on "acquiring a certain kind of looseness—contingency is a good word—an ability to adapt and respond very directly to the urban environment."[19]

Following the success of the Idea Stores and MCAD, in which Adjaye proved his ability to generate designs that are embedded in a sense of place, he was invited to conceive two new libraries for neighborhoods in Washington, D.C. These projects, completed in 2012, were envisioned as community centers, and their distinctive designs have been recognized as a significant step in improving the city's educational infrastructure. The Francis A. Gregory Library, in the southeast of the city, stands on the edge of woodlands. It is a jewel box of a building, with a floating steel roof that visually extends the structure, connects it to the surrounding landscape, and helps to control sun exposure. The rich color palette of the interiors (deep greens, yellows, and reds) and the diagonal solid/void pattern of the external walls—heightened by the use of Douglas fir plywood internally, and reflected in the shadows on the walls and floors—were also chosen for their relevance to what Adjaye describes as the lush savanna-like quality of Washington, D.C. The generous use of glazing, which allows dappled light to fill the interior, further connects the structure to the geographic terrain.

The William O. Lockridge Library in Washington Highlands in southwest Washington, D.C., is a more complex structure that makes equally strong connections to its surroundings. (Fig 10) Set on a sloping site in a residential area, the library is composed of a series of interconnected wings. They "pick up on the local vernacular of garages, porches and spare rooms attached to old brick houses," and the agglomerated arrangement fans out over the site, taking advantage of the different elevations created by the slope, with the components connected by a series of elevated passageways.[20] The informal clustering of linked pavilions is also reminiscent of the village clusters that Adjaye had previously photographed in Africa. The volumetric massing emphasizes the library's role as a civic structure, and the continuity of this complex composition is underpinned by the use of vertical wooden ribs that repeat at intervals across the surfaces of the wings, visually tying them together. As in the Idea Stores, the Washington libraries make tactical use of the placement of windows. For example, a promontory in the William O. Lockridge Library overlooks the public space carved out at ground level, which is used for events such as yard sales and family activities that further activate the relationship between the building and the community.

Adjaye's understanding of the importance of material choices, formal decisions, programmatic needs, and the demands of environmental conditions has been honed equally through observation and fact-finding as through theoretical inquiry. He draws references from across geographical and cultural borders. This ability to assimilate diverse ideas and influences was

18.   Nikos Papastergiadis, *Cosmopolitanism and Culture* (Polity, 2012), p. 89.

19.   Horst Rutsch, "Trying to Look at Architecture Differently," *UN Chronicle* 43, 2 (July–Aug. 2006), p. 46.

20.   Russell Crader, Adjaye Associates Project Director, quoted in Michael Webb, "Two Libraries, One Architect," in *Another Architect* 41 (Dec.–Jan. 2012–13), p. 151.

(Fig 07) MOSCOW SCHOOL OF MANAGEMENT SKOLKOVO
Moscow, 2006-10

Ways of Building
Zoë Ryan

(Fig 08) El Lissitzky (Russian, 1890–1941)
Drawing of *Wolkenbügel* on Strastnoy Boulevard,
Moscow, 1925

(Fig 09) Konstantin Melnikov (Russian, 1890–1974)
Melnikov House, Moscow, 1927–29

no doubt developed during his upbringing and early childhood moving around Africa and the Middle East before his family settled in London when he was a teenager. More recently he conducted an eleven-year study of the architecture of Africa, documenting buildings in every capital city. The study, called African Metropolitan Architecture, has informed much of his subsequent architectural practice, which has been defined by a continued interest in developing designs with universal qualities that speak to diverse audiences and yet are "specific to place" and attentive to their context.

While developing the libraries, Adjaye won the commission for the Smithsonian's National Museum of African American History and Culture (NMAAHC), to be sited on the National Mall, the cultural heart of the city and the nation—a project of immense international stature and importance. Situated at the end of the Mall, adjacent to the Washington Monument, the NMAAHC site can be approached from all four sides. This prompted Adjaye to borrow from the classical Palladian tradition of a symmetrical plan that looks equally significant from all angles. Other references, however, are taken from Africa. The tiered form of the building, reminiscent of a crown, was inspired by the work of Yoruba sculptor Olowe of Ise, who carved veranda posts incorporating caryatids with capitals in the shape of inverted ziggurats in the late nineteenth and early twentieth centuries in what is now Nigeria (see p. 69).

The bronze-coated facade uses a material steeped in African tradition, exemplified in the exquisite Benin bronzes from Nigeria. But it is also inspired by more local contexts—the work of some of the first African American slaves freed in the American South, who contributed to the visual iconography of towns such as Charleston and New Orleans through the architectural detailing of their bronze balustrades and screens. For the facade treatment of the NMAAHC, Adjaye's team creatively transformed these sources. They retraced the earlier designs (themselves derived from forms found in nature) and employed parametric modeling tools to generate a geometric pattern that constitutes a contemporary reinterpretation. The facade not only provides a stunning visual reference but, through shifts in the pattern's density across the surface of the building, offers environmental benefits and mitigates solar gain. Here, as in the Moscow School of Management Skolkovo, pattern provides an additional register through which to locate and read the building.

In Adjaye's public projects the relationship between the inside and outside is one of the most considered aspects of the design—and the most significant for making structures that engage with their sites and encourage public interaction. The porch, a device he frequently employs (at the Bernie Grant Arts Centre in London, for example), also hearkens back to centuries-old architectural traditions. But in the Smithsonian museum it appears as a feat of engineering as ambitious as those in projects by architects such as Gordon Bunshaft and I. M. Pei, whose work also addresses the National Mall. Located on the south entrance of the NMAAHC, spanning two hundred feet and suspended from two columns, this is no simple loggia. Instead it creates what Adjaye refers to as an "adjustment space" that transitions visitors from the street to the inside of the building, announcing their arrival and reinforcing the momentous significance and celebratory nature of this museum. The Central Hall, immediately inside the building, is the primary space for reflecting on the significance of the history and culture that the structure represents. Conceived as a public gathering space, it is a place where people can "hover" before deciding which part of the museum to visit.[21] The continuous curve of the ceiling, made from vertical timber posts of varying lengths (a symbol of a people coming together), both distinguishes and softens the space. In multiple ways, the Smithsonian museum demonstrates Adjaye's belief that public buildings should be extensions of the urban frame.

21.   Adjaye, in conversation with the author, July 22, 2013.

LOOKING TO THE FUTURE

The development of Adjaye's work has followed a similar trajectory in several locations. In London, his first independent buildings were relatively small studio-houses within walking distance of his then-office. Taking leads from the history and culture of the area, it was not long before he was designing public buildings, dispersed over a somewhat wider area but still within close range of the office. In the United States the thread that connected his early projects was that of contemporary art. His first commission, in 2003, was for a double-studio building on an infill site in Brooklyn, known as Pitch Black. The experience of developing this project, together with a number of collaborations with artists, underpinned the presentations that resulted in his winning the commissions for LN House in Denver, Colorado, and MCAD, his first public building in North America. A practical involvement in Africa has developed over a longer period, in which he undertook African Metropolitan Architecture. His first building there, Nkron, in Ghana, is a house that celebrates both the scale of the African landscape and the history of modernism on the continent.

The second African project, the Alara Concept Store in Lagos, Nigeria, completed in 2014, involves the location of an innovative retail facility in a residential area. But the majority of African projects in development in Adjaye's office are on a significantly larger scale: Roman Ridge Gardens, a climate-friendly apartment building in Accra, Ghana, and Hallmark Towers, the mixed-use conversion of an older concrete-framed building in Johannesburg, South Africa, for example. He is also involved on a long-term basis in master-plan projects in Libreville, Gabon, and Kampala, Uganda, and for Petronia, a new technology city near Takoradi, about 140 miles west of Accra. Adjaye is now working in two of the six geographic terrains he identified in African Metropolitan Architecture. Extending his climate- and culture-based methodology to yet another continent, he is currently responsible for several projects in Asia: Al Kahraba Street in Doha, Qatar;[Fig 11] a commercial-cultural hybrid, the Aïshti Foundation, in Beirut, Lebanon,[Fig 12] which will be the first to be completed; the Varanasi Silkweaving Facility in Varanasi, India; and the Art Campus Tel Aviv, in Tel Aviv, Israel,[Fig 13] where a theater, dance studios, and a community building will collectively define a new public space in a neglected area of the city. His first project in Asia was Nanjing House, commissioned in 2004 but only completed in 2012.

As his projects demonstrate, Adjaye remains faithful to ideas he has tested and developed from one project to the next. His systematic method has enabled him to refine his approach while enlarging the scope and scale of his output. Committed to creating projects that resonate internationally as much as they respond to local imperatives, his designs also meet societal needs, and his interest in reinterpreting standard typologies is always evident. He emphasizes the value of the built frame that is normally subsumed into our daily lives, taken for granted and forgotten. He also aims to establish new relationships between architecture and other artistic disciplines and social practices, and to create alliances that foster inventive outcomes. Adjaye continues to design architecture that makes "meaning of where we are."[22] He draws inspiration from Western and non-Western traditions that help him find appropriate responses to climate, lifestyle, and visual and material sensibilities, generating outcomes that are uniquely his.

Just as Adjaye learned from the Smithsons that the "design of a building . . . cannot be evolved outside its context," he has remained critical of contemporary architectural discourses that are divorced from the social implications of daily life.[23] He looks to strengthen social and cultural alignments and borrow vernacular references that will help engage users. Adjaye is,

22.   Ibid.

23.   Alison and Peter Smithson, *Without Rhetoric: An Architectural Aesthetic, 1955–1972* (MIT Press, 1974), p. 85.

(Fig 10) WILLIAM O. LOCKRIDGE LIBRARY
Washington, D.C., 2008-12

(Fig 11) AL KAHRABA STREET
Doha, Qatar, designed 2010
Al Kahraba Street, rendering

(Fig 12) AÏSHTI FOUNDATION
Beirut, Lebanon, 2012—15
Waterfront plaza, model

(Fig 13) ART CAMPUS TEL AVIV
Tel Aviv, Israel, designed 2013
Entrance to new urban square, rendering

however, at an interesting stage in his career. Having led his studio for almost fifteen years and with close to fifty built projects to his name, he is in the process of adapting the bespoke quality of his early work to the needs of a range of large-scale commissions, in which he must balance design details with larger concerns related to issues such as site specificity, history, culture, charged political and social situations, and environmental concerns. As his projects grow in scope and scale, he must manage an increasingly complex network of clients, as well as the growing expectations of the public, while grappling with his own beliefs and with questions about architecture's ability to be an agent for change. What is clear, though, is his unwavering determination to respond to these challenges. "We are in an age in which we need to rethink what architecture does best, how it makes sense to people," he has noted, asking, "Is architecture just solving problems?"[24] His response is neither surprising nor unexpected, and signals his continued commitment to questioning the role of architecture in today's society: "Architecture is about where we are, how we are, and where we want to go."[25]

24. David Adjaye, *When Is Now?*, video recording of a lecture delivered at the Graduate School of Architecture, Planning and Preservation, Columbia University, New York, Jan. 25, 2012.

25. Ibid.

SM

MONU

ALL
MENTS

THE WASHINGTON COLLECTION
For Knoll, New York, 2013
The Washington Corona coffee table

From early in his career, David Adjaye has found opportunities to
develop his architectural thinking in situations where many of the
technical expectations associated with conventional buildings do not
apply. This is not to say that the pavilions, furniture, and vases
designed on this basis are in any way private studies: regardless of
size, they have the capacity to occupy public space, and this accounts
for their monumental presence and their ability to engage the eye.
Standing in a variety of locations, they provide a point of focus,
a measure of scale, a spatial experience, and a sequence of views—all
of a kind that did not previously exist there. They are protopublic
buildings, gathering places in which to reflect on the state of the
surrounding city. Often taking the form of protected platforms, they
suggest that Adjaye is primarily concerned with making spaces that
establish new relationships between people, places, and institutions.

The connections between these "small monuments" and Adjaye's
buildings are rich and varied. In Shada, a pavilion designed with the
artist Henna Nadeem, the perforations of the Corten steel roof produce
a shadow pattern of London plane tree leaves on the ground. This
illustrates Adjaye's interest in incorporating the effects of natural
phenomena within buildings: in the Nobel Peace Center, for example,
the backlit glass walls of the culminating space, the Nobel Field,
represent a sky. Asymmetric Chamber and Length × Width × Height make
use of everyday materials to construct arcade-like spaces, and
Lost House and the library floors of the Idea Stores are their progeny.
Horizon, on the other hand, recombines the volumes of a previously
designed building—the Stephen Lawrence Centre—in a more compressed
composition. The Monoforms furniture line merges the prow-like corners
in some of the early public buildings with an ongoing interest
in geological forms to investigate the type of oblique geometries
seen in the Aïshti Foundation building. In its shape and internal
composition, Sclera demonstrates an interest in Baroque geometries
involving the circle and its derivatives, a line of inquiry pursued
in later pavilions and in spaces such as the Central Hall of the
National Museum of African American History and Culture. With their
stick construction and enveloping spaces, several of the pavilions
suggest both caves and birds' nests: nature's models for human
construction, according to the ancient Roman architect Vitruvius.

The pavilions embody the core of Adjaye's concerns as an
architect. They are resolutely low tech, in most cases based on the
gathering of simple components into the larger assemblies—floor, walls,
and roof—that constitute each structure. The simultaneous legibility
of process and result speaks of the time and circumstances in which
the pavilions were created: nothing is hidden and other possibilities
are not precluded. One composition contains the seeds of another;
each responds equally attentively to its situation. A similar tendency
is visible in the pavilions' references to key developments in the
history of architecture: the gathering under a tree, the shaded arcade,
the raised platform, the intimate threshold, the framed view.
These moments are the subject of the pavilions, and they take on new
resonance in Adjaye's buildings.

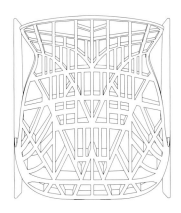

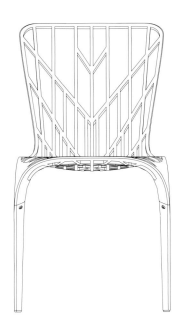

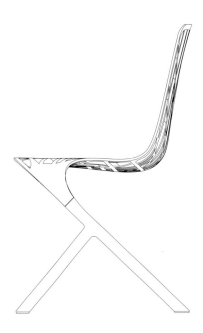

THE WASHINGTON COLLECTION
For Knoll, New York, 2013
Plan and elevations of the Washington Skin chair

RIVER READING ROOM
Gwangju, South Korea, 2013
Street-level view

View from riverside park showing
indented bookshelves

EPHEMEROPTERAE
Vienna, 2012

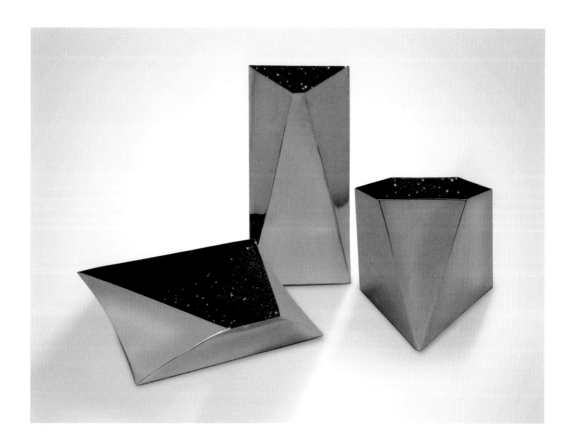

STAR COLLECTION
Milan, 2012

GENESIS
Miami, 2011
Exterior view

Detail of suspended ceiling

SPECERE
Kielder Water and Forest Park, United Kingdom, 2009
Exterior view

Framed view of landscape

SCLERA
London, 2008
Entrance

View showing side opening and ceiling

HORIZON
London, 2007, and Rome, 2008
Interior view showing slotted construction

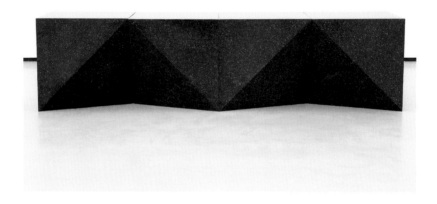

MONOFORMS
London, 2007
Type II-Petra

Type I-Ginza

LENGTH x WIDTH x HEIGHT
London, 2007
Interior view, with floor sloping downwards

ASYMMETRIC CHAMBER
Manchester, United Kingdom, 2003, and New York, 2005
The central space

A side space

SHADA
London, 1999
View showing benches and tables

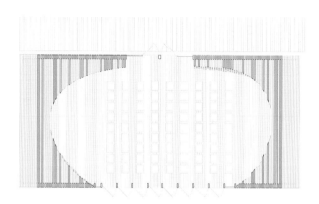

THE CHAPEL
Chicago, 2015
View showing entrance, rendering

Floor plan

SHADA
London, 1999
Detail of roof

THE LESSON OF AFRICA
DAVID ADJAYE

(Fig 01) The towers of Le Plateau, 2005
Abidjan, Côte d'Ivoire

The Lesson of Africa
David Adjaye

(Fig 02) Place des Cinéastes, 2006
Ouagadougou, Burkina Faso

(Fig 03) Street facade, 2013
Harlem, New York

My book on the architecture and urbanism of the continent's capitals, <u>African Metropolitan Architecture</u>, was published in 2011, more than ten years after my first study visit to one of these cities. I had felt that I needed to act on my longstanding interest in the continent and in cities, which I'd had since I first started to study architecture. As a student, it was clear that the relationship between buildings and cities demonstrated certain possibilities, which I could then visualize back in the urban context: the city became the laboratory for thinking through ideas and scenarios. The Africa study allowed me to develop a particular overview and to improve my understanding of other cities and of how architecture could be made. I wanted to look at the fundamentals of the African city, to understand the issues that are currently in play, beyond the continent's historical and architectural traditions. The climate and landscape of Africa are so varied that there you can really feel how powerfully geography and culture shape place.

I first grasped the connection between geography and architecture when I was an exchange student in Kyoto, Japan. The Africa study allowed me to see why that connection is significant and gave me confidence in what I am doing. It was more or less autobiographical to start with (I visited places I knew from childhood) but once I began to look at the information and share it with others, it was clear that I needed to transcend autobiography to do justice to it. If the study was to be conclusive, to serve as a basis for a wider discourse, I needed to understand the full scope of the subject and to analyze the situation across the entire continent. Now that <u>African Metropolitan Architecture</u> is complete, it allows me to be more explicit about my concerns and how my studio should approach them. In the book, the photographs of each city are grouped under three main headings—civic, commercial, and residential—that cover the range of urban building types. I follow that division in the reflections below.

CIVIC

The public buildings in a city exhibit a range of architectural gestures and also relate to the state of development and the economic situation. They represent the public life of the city; they describe the key attitudes in the city and how it chooses to project them into the world.(Fig 02) Understanding how these attitudes have been articulated is a key part of my approach. This is why I examine the arsenal of parts that are employed to articulate "civicness" even more than the social context, although that is also important. The way these parts are deployed under different geographic conditions is deeply fascinating and, in terms of design, my normal preference is to work toward some sort of balance with the existing references.

The expression of the public buildings I designed in London refers to the neighborhoods in which they are located, and to the city in general. In siting a project, I like to pick up on geometries or textures that are not immediately apparent. If there are nuances to the sense of place, I'm interested in bringing out those qualities, and there is often a reference to something simple that anchors the project in its setting. It could be anything from the reflections of water (the dappled nature of water that we explored in the metal facade of the Stephen Lawrence Centre) to the relationship with the nearby market stalls in the Idea Store buildings. I deliberately choose references of this kind because of their intrinsic weakness, as that gives me a great many options in concretizing them, increasing their status in the composition of the urban environment. This is important in terms of trying to create an emotional feeling of inclusion. At the same time, and operating in parallel, a more abstract strategy always drives the way I see things. It concerns the compositional relationship between the conditions I am dealing with, and I might see this in a particular textile, the geometry of an artifact, or even a basket that suggests how interlocking systems produce certain forms. There is a world knowledge, a place knowledge, and a context knowledge: the success of a project depends on bringing them together in a single complexity.

The projects my studio and I have developed in New York and Washington, D.C., are closely tuned to the specificity of their locations. The design of Sugar Hill in Harlem, New York, for example, responds to the site's surroundings, both past and present. A hybrid building, it has apartments in the upper section and an early childhood center and children's museum in the base. In the nineteenth century, the Sugar Hill neighborhood was an area of farms, where people could escape the density of the rest of Manhattan and enjoy the cool breezes. I was very taken with the memory of this bucolic idyll but, in our design, we had to recognize the current density of Sugar Hill and the urbanity of its structures. In the upper section of our building, I wanted to work with the idea of masonry architecture, but without the restrictions on the size and position of openings that come with using a traditional material.[Fig 03] Employing precast concrete panels allowed us to set up a rhythm of small and large windows that speaks of a range of internal spaces without actually representing them on the exterior. At street level, in contrast, the facade is continuously glazed, giving views deep into the shared zone where the use patterns of the building intersect. Two details lock the Sugar Hill project into its context. A quirky brownstone building stands close to the site; its stepped facade is a response to the landscape of the area, as it falls away toward the Harlem River.[Fig 04] The upper facade of our building repeats this feature, establishing a family resemblance with the older buildings. Second, we embossed a black rose pattern on the surface of the concrete panels—a reference to upper Harlem having had beautiful rose gardens in the nineteenth century and thus a reminder of its idyllic past. This is not a literal representation of roses but rather a light-responsive drawing: the roses come to life when the sun shines on them; at other times they are less visible and the building looks more austere and somber. This is a project about Harlem physically, Harlem as a historical idea, and Harlem now.

The Smithsonian Institution's National Museum of African American History and Culture (NMAAHC) in Washington, D.C., is one of the few examples in my work where the external expression includes references to history. Conceptually it is about the identity of a marginalized group that has played, and continues to play, a very significant role in the United States. The National Mall represents the body of the nation and the new building will complete that image. Architecturally, the project continues the modernist discourse of Gordon Bunshaft's Hirshhorn Museum and I. M. Pei's East Building but, in its superstructure, it refers to a sculpture by the early-twentieth-century Yoruba sculptor Olowe of Ise.[Fig 05] It was a joy to discover this sculpture because it served as a lightning rod for a range of issues that otherwise seemed very disparate and complex. The form was so powerful that it allowed us to bypass the problems of intellectualizing what the project should be about. It concretized the design process: it was a crown, it was a column capital, it had a pyramid reference, and despite the passage of time, it represented the aesthetic world of the Africans who were brought to America as slaves. The pyramid is actually inverted, creating an upward trajectory, and when we conducted a survey, we discovered that it is a form that is associated with uplift and is etched in the collective memory. With the pyramid pointing the other way, it represents death and the ground, but in Washington, D.C., we are using it the other way, up, as a celebration—the provisional conclusion to a long history.

COMMERCIAL

The buildings grouped in <u>African Metropolitan Architecture</u> under the heading "commercial" are extraordinarily varied, from sleek office towers to rudimentary shops with protective canopies. These are the buildings that articulate what is left of the public realm when you take away traffic and all the other activities occurring there. (Fig 06) It is no irony that when I make commercial buildings, they become quite formless and extended, so that they can absorb as much as possible of what is going on around them. Their plans are very loose and sometimes rather nebulous, but they create complex sectional relationships, and that is very deliberate. They are relevant to the city as tools to provide a more performative landscape. You can see this in the <u>One Berkeley Street</u> project in London. The facade makes a public urban landscape that is absolutely deferential to the street, and the spatial infrastructure of the building is developed from local precedents.

Commercial architecture is usually focused on function and efficiency but, for me, these are not the most significant criteria. The most successful commercial spaces are increasingly those that enrich the performance of public life, whether by permitting citizens to see one another on the street (including seeing the different generations together) or by creating new landscapes in places where there is very little stimulus. Commercial buildings have the capacity to offer new directions because they operate within a timeline that suggests that they can be remade. This is the spirit in which we designed the <u>Aïshti Foundation</u> in Beirut, Lebanon, which is a commercial-cultural hybrid. The site is on a freeway that is one of the most beautiful trajectories out of Beirut, toward Byblos and other important cities. On the other side of the site is the ocean, which has always been inaccessible here. My whole premise was to turn a commercial building into a frame for understanding the landscape and where you are within it. We employed a system that acts as a noise reflector, tilting and bouncing the sounds of the road away, while creating a series of cuts that pulls you through to the sea. The building happens to be a retail mall, but the final destination is a new waterfront plaza, and the view toward it is continuously reframed. The same concept informs the organization of the art institution that occupies one end of the building. The color of the protective latticework refers to the red-tiled roofs of Beirut's historic masonry buildings. It is the color that my father always mentions when he talks about his time in the city.

In the <u>Alara Concept Store</u> in Lagos, Nigeria, we aimed to make commercial space a destination in its own right. (Fig 10) In West Africa there is a great deal of informal selling that happens right on the street, but this project was about creating a retail experience that is worth driving to, so it is conceived as three villas in a landscape. The feeling is like arriving at a grand house: there are gardens and shaded spaces between the buildings, and you can meander through them. Entering the first of the three structures, you realize that it does not have normal floors: it is basically a folding landscape that leads to a pavilion on the roof, and the view tells you where you are in the city. Ascending to that moment is the essence of the project, and the terraces on that ascent are the moments of commerce.

The Lesson of Africa
David Adjaye

(Fig 04) Stepped facade,
Saint Nicholas Avenue, 2011
Sugar Hill, Harlem, New York

Markets and street traders are an integral part of everyday life in Africa. (Fig 07) The informal sector is the product of a very resourceful entrepreneurial class. They aim to take hold of their destiny by succeeding in the gray economy in the face of weak government. It is a significant phenomenon because it bespeaks citizens' desire to establish their own infrastructure. This effort creates an architectural space that is not just fly-by-night but provides a platform for these entrepreneurs and their families to establish themselves in society. It is a space that has an important role in incubating new enterprises, and I see this as part of the role of the city. In my photographs, I recorded how informal activity locates itself in urban spaces where it can flourish: busy pedestrian thoroughfares, forecourts of imposing buildings, and street corners with wide pavements. I am very concerned with understanding the architectural implications of this phenomenon.

RESIDENTIAL

I am equally fascinated by the way cities develop residential typologies that respond to climate and culture: tower houses in the medina in Algiers, Morocco; houses with breeze-catching terraces in Nouakchott, Mauritania; mud-brick compounds in Ouagadougou, Burkina Faso; hillside clusters in Antananarivo, Madagascar; apartment buildings looking toward the ocean in Luanda, Angola; and shady suburbs in Harare, Zimbabwe. The way in which each home takes its place in a larger group contributes to the sense of retreat, regardless of whether the neighborhood is in the center of the city or on the periphery. The work-life balance we have in the twenty-first century suggests that, more than ever, we need the basic building typologies—civic, commercial, and residential— to take on specific qualities that give their users the sense of a larger rhythm operating across the city. This is not a matter of building houses in garden suburbs, but it does depend on understanding residential typologies and how they create a sense of rest before entering the public realm. When you consider a cross section of the different building types in the African city, you see it affords a range of experiences that, taken together, are fulfilling. (Fig 01)

I articulate individual houses on a different basis than dense projects. In the houses, the architecture is opaque and inward looking, giving a sense of interiority. In the case of multistory projects, the spectacle of the public realm is more interesting—it becomes a landscape. In Roman Ridge Gardens, in Accra, Ghana, the entrance sequences take you through a garden in an intimation of the experience of being on an upper floor. Once inside, the architecture is about these glazed walls that frame the city—the home as a theater seat to an urban landscape. Externally, such buildings are somber and quite abstract, like pieces of infrastructure. I see them as structural frames in which each house occupies a specific position, with its own conditions and experiences. These buildings are a new concern and I am very interested in the relationship between their external appearance and the way in which the experience of the interior reverses the initial perception of the exterior.

In African Metropolitan Architecture, I included examples of traditional huts and their groupings. (Fig 08) As rural populations migrate to the city and the huts themselves become less relevant as a building type, their forms begin to take on an archaeological power, and are a possible reference point in places where the indigenous context has been wiped clean by colonialism and post-colonialism. Such archetypes can be layered into contemporary forms, where they can resonate with the psyche of the population. This is how I read the circular tower of the Kenyatta Conference Centre, completed by Karl Hendrik Nostvik and David Mutiso in Nairobi, Kenya, in 1972. Our proposal for a cluster of ten thirteen-story towers in the Nakawa district of Kampala is a reworking of the cone-like structure that supports the roofs of traditional huts in Uganda.

CLIMATE & LIGHT

In photographing the building typologies of African cities, my underlying concern was to understand the role of geography and climate in the urban environment. To this end, the cities are grouped in six geographic terrains: the Maghreb, Desert, the Sahel, Savanna and Grassland, Forest, and Mountain and Highveld. Examples of certain building types can be found in several locations across the continent, but their architectural expression is particular to each geographic terrain, arcaded commercial structures being a case in point. As I visited more cities, I found that climate began to play an increasingly significant role in my architecture, not just for how it shapes practical responses, but because it shapes the culture of a place and how people relate to one another. Knowledge and democracy are at the root of how I present my work, and how the work is articulated in context. In London's Idea Store Whitechapel, for instance, we needed to protect the south facade from the sun but chose to do so in a way that creates an in-between space that is both diaphanous and luminous. I now realize that this solution was driven by a desire to extend the building fabric and create a sense of comfort, rather than by the simple need to deal with the sun. Since then it has become clear that in most situations double-skin construction probably offers the most profound response when looking at climate and its impact.

Climate also determines the strength and quality of light in a place, which have become important factors in my work, as evidenced by the Museum of Contemporary Art Denver in Denver, Colorado, and Nkron in Ghana. In the house everything is about seeing the light without it falling on you, so the interior world and the external world are practically equal, due to how the floor and roof slabs extend outward. Only reflected light reaches the interior and, compared with the outside, the atmosphere is soft and comfortable. This strategy is based on the location's relationship to the equator, the position of the sun, and the way it bears down on the land. In Denver, you are away from the equator but very high up, so the sun is relatively weak but there is plenty of light—more than you want in an art museum. The building we designed is intended to channel the light, like a lens. At the center of the site, we created a T-shaped aperture, which draws light deep into the section and illuminates the diagram of the building. In the galleries, we reflect and refract the light through clerestory windows. They harvest the natural light so that the spaces can function with only limited use of artificial light.

Depending on the latitude and the way in which the sun works in a specific zone, I am either working with an architecture of heavenly, zenithal perforations or with reflective surfaces that bounce indirect light into the interior. This is not a matter of style: it is a response to place. The London work was always about the zenithal—light from above—because it struck me that this was the only way to create maximum luminosity and radiance. I had to decide whether to use windows or skylights, and I chose to make roof systems or clerestories—multiple skylights or horizontal windows in elevated positions. That was the defining goal and is the reason why Elektra House in London is like it is—it emphasizes everything to do with the zenithal. If I were to make that house in Accra, Ghana, I would not have zenithal openings because of the strength of the light. When I am working close to the equator, it is always about setting up layers that protect the interior, setting up a kind of darkness that looks to the light.

Lost House, also in London, tested the idea that darkness could endow materials with a certain texturality. The reduced palette comes from having to stretch the budget. I basically spent the budget on creating the zenithal light wells, which were very expensive, and I wanted to create a textural background that would be responsive to the dappled light. There was no opportunity to set up conventional elevations and I was resistant to peppering the roof with skylights, so I decided to work with the introverted nature of the site. To maximize that quality was very interesting but it was an unusual operation in a northern climate.

(Fig 05) Olowe of Ise (Yoruba, c. 1875–c. 1938)
Painted wood veranda post with caryatid, before 1938
Obagi Akoko, Ondo, Nigeria
Museum Fünf Kontinente, Munich

The Lesson of Africa
David Adjaye

(Fig 06) Commercial facades, 2009
Kampala, Uganda

(Fig 07) Vegetable stall, 2010
Mbabane, Swaziland

MATERIALITY

Despite the wealth of materials available in Africa, buildings are not usually materially expansive. There is often more emphasis on the articulation of surfaces, and I was fascinated to see that the selection of materials was not the only means to determine the materiality of a structure.(Fig 09) Before the Africa study, I was interested in discovering materials that would create new collisions to address the questions and emotions of the present moment. The laminated timber sections that stiffen the external walls in London's Idea Stores are an example of this: they look like normal timber but are in fact waste timber that has been recycled. Over the course of the study, I became more concerned with the rearticulation of the familiar. In the Francis A. Gregory Library in Washington, D.C., for instance, the palette of materials is absolutely familiar but the relationship between them is shifted, and the way in which they are recontextualized is a key component of the design. In the Central Hall of the NMAAHC, which otherwise employs noble materials such as bronze and steel, the ceiling will be constructed of pine—the same timber that is used to construct regular houses.

In African Metropolitan Architecture there are many examples of buildings with strongly patterned facades, where the pattern comes from how the elements have been shaped and assembled. Searching for patterns is like searching for the building blocks of my projects. But it is not about finding just any sort of pattern: it is primarily about setting up a constructive relationship between the different systems that I am considering in relation to the specific demands of the brief and the place. When I look at brickwork, for instance, it is not the bricks I am interested in but the lattice created by the horizontal and vertical joints, which tells me how the bricks were put together. This approach offers an immediate basis for understanding the relationship between things, and that comes into play in the double-skin arrangement, where I decouple the need for the internal function to be expressed on the exterior. It allows me to deal with the forces of harsh climate, or to decouple the internal function from the expression of the exterior.

Pattern plays a significant role in the Art Campus Tel Aviv, a hybrid complex in which Platonic forms interact with a system of screens. The design is about the way these elements dissolve into each other; it is about a double program in which each of the solids has a singular purpose, while the screens draw the solids into a continuous whole. There is a layering and a latticing, and you do not see any windows unless I need to articulate something very specific. All the other window openings are behind these latticeworks of stone or precast concrete. When there is a complexity that I want to reduce to a silhouette—or to the profile of the form—pattern is a useful device. It is a key component of the NMAAHC because, if you remove the external screen, you are left with a highly complex object. The patterned screen is the device that reasserts the singular purpose of the building and mediates between its internal complexity and the urban condition. The silhouette represents the soul of the building. It is the basis on which you discover the project; it invites you to connect with this new experience.

<u>The Lesson of Africa</u>
David Adjaye

(Fig 08) Tomb for four Buganda kings, 2009
Kasubi, Kampala, Uganda

PLACE & GEOGRAPHY

Visiting fifty-two African cities, I could not ignore the impact of colonialism, but in the study I was primarily concerned with its legacy for the present. Colonial architecture is effective in climate moderation and in the way in which it deploys specific devices, such as planning grids, to understand place.(Fig 12) Rational grids, hypergrids, and distorting grids: they come together to produce the rich and varied conditions that I recorded in my photographs. I employ all of these systems in our master-planning projects in Africa: the efficient grids of the French, with their master-planned quartiers, in which you always know where you are; the garden suburbs, combining landscape and built form, that were introduced by the English; the looser grids of the Portuguese, which are rational to a degree but flexible enough to respond to the local terrain. Grids can create a series of thresholds and a hierarchy of scale. If a place has an important symbolic role, I can increase the scale for larger urban ideas and still maintain a sense of intimacy in the residential areas. I would say that the whole point of employing different grids is the moment when you make the patchwork, creating new fusions between the dense and the bucolic, the generic and the symbolic.(Fig 11) These points of change and hybridity complete the system.

Colonial buildings were constructed as symbols of power, but my book argues that eventually they take on an indigenous identity and represent a critical period in the continent's history. Their original purpose was to create a climatic envelope where the Other—in this context —could find protection in an alien environment. They were machines to cool down the colonizers and had to set up very specific scenarios to moderate the natural conditions. This architecture may be questionable in other respects but, in terms of climatic response, it is highly effective.

I was in the final stage of the Africa study when we were first invited to work in Washington, D.C., and I think my knowledge of the tropics informed my understanding of its context. As in colonial cities, the central composition in the American capital was constructed in a relatively short period of time, which gives it a powerful singularity. This was a quality I felt I understood: the immediate possibility of reading the city. African cities are in a moment of creating their identities, and in Washington I saw how the identity of the place had been laid out in a way that was highly accessible.

In the global context, architecture can create a bridge between otherwise divergent conditions. The Varanasi Silkweaving Facility in Varanasi, India, is intended to do this. The project employs the commercialism of Western culture to ensure the continuation of a handweaving tradition in a context where it is under threat. This involves Hindus and Muslims working together in a program that has international roots, and the use of architecture as a device to negotiate these conflicting paradigms of commercialism and craft. It is about creating a place of empowerment between different worlds, a meeting place that will support an ongoing dialogue. I am always concerned that my buildings should feel equally comfortable to all stakeholders, whatever their personal concerns. My approach is to make places that offer new experiences to everyone. I think it is more forward-looking to set up a scenario that sits above the familiarity of the different groups: a counterpoint where everyone is happy to meet.

The charged compression in the Central Hall of the NMAAHC creates just such a condition. This is the premier space in the building, and it is designed as an urban room for the city, a place for people to congregate, whether individually or in groups. It also forms a shortcut from the National Mall to the White House, so that people who are doing the traditional tour can shorten the route by passing through the building. The structure welcomes everyone, and the sense of uplift that comes from the silhouette of the Corona is reinforced by the section of the suspended ceiling in the

The Lesson of Africa
David Adjaye

(Fig 09) Central Bank of West African States, 2006
Bamako, Mali
View showing articulated brick surfaces

(Fig 10) ALARA CONCEPT STORE
Lagos, Nigeria, 2011-14
Gallery and offices on left, concept
store at center, and hotel on right

The Lesson of Africa
David Adjaye

(Fig 11) GOVERNMENT QUARTER MASTER PLAN
Libreville, Gabon, designed 2012
The Emancipation Pavilion sited
on the cross axis, rendering

(Fig 12) Grid-based development, 2009
Dar es Salaam, Tanzania

Central Hall. It is also the point of departure for the floors below ground level, where the permanent collection and the main auditorium are located, and for the black box galleries for temporary exhibitions in the Corona. These are the polemics of the display strategy: one option that is carefully considered and atmospheric—entombing a historic trajectory—and a more neutral option that is open to evolution and change. Because the upper galleries are self-contained, it is important to ensure that people know exactly where they are in the building. With this in mind, each of these spaces has a distinctive threshold condition. Leaving the uppermost gallery, you can see the sweep of the Mall; from the middle gallery, your view is focused on the Washington Monument by a lens-like window, and exiting the lower level, you are in a canyon of light.

In conceiving of socially inclusive spaces, I refer to various systems that animate and talk about notions of the public. How that plays out in detail varies from project to project. In the Art Campus Tel Aviv, the whole idea is to restage the public, back to the public. The buildings are clustered around a central space, a raised stage, which is also a response to a change of level on the site. On each side of this space we framed gateways through existing historic buildings; they set up several landscape trajectories, with our buildings serving as anchors. These are devices of a kind you see in the theater, but here they are part of the civic realm and their purpose is to create an awareness of the nature of public space. We extend this thinking into each building, while the campus as a whole is intended to register in the urban composition of Tel Aviv. The systems that I employ in these public projects are informed by my interest in geography as a driver of distinctive spatial typologies. These typologies mutate and shift when they move to other places, encounter other cultures in unfamiliar locales, and, as a result, acquire new depth and meaning.

For me, the geographic basis for architecture is always apparent if you know how to look for it. Sometimes it does not appear to be the core consideration—in places that are highly developed, for instance—but I realize it is a constant presence and the best architects always home in on it. I was recently in Helsinki and looked at some of Alvar Aalto's buildings. You cannot help but notice that he must have been preoccupied by the geography of the place. Yes, he was playing the classical nuances in certain aspects of his architecture, but his core inventions were a direct response to this Nordic, glacial place. His contemporaries were concerned about style and a certain kind of symbolism, but he broke from that because of his emotional understanding of the place he was working in. My intention in having studios on three continents is to develop an organization that has this kind of awareness in several places. Originating from a single body of ideas, our output needs to be fully responsive to each context. I see this as the program for Adjaye Associates over the next decades.

LIV
SPA

NG
CES

NKRON
Ghana, 2008-12

David Adjaye's residential projects are essentially private commissions,
developed in close conversation with his clients. But the various site
conditions and the singularity of each client's expectations have been
a fruitful combination for exploring new spatial concepts and forms of
construction. Dirty House is the first of his projects with an outward-
looking roof pavilion, supported on a more self-contained volume.
The spaces of Lost House are strung along a route that is three times as
long as the overall length of the building, suggesting that movement is
an asset, not a drawback. Silverlight shows how spaces within a steel-
frame structure can meet specific requirements if lined with highly
differentiated sets of materials. Seven explores the materiality of
cast concrete, both from the point of view of building in the city and in
terms of living with its textures at close quarters. Nkron, on the other
hand, employs pigmented concrete as a geometric extension of a sweeping
landscape, in Adjaye's first project to engage with the scale of Africa.
The Asem Pa, Make It Right houses are strictly layered: a raised ground
floor in case of flooding, an intermediate floor hosting the main living
spaces, and a shaded deck open to the breeze and the surrounding views.
Case Study Housing employs the timber technology of Sunken House to
assemble homes of different sizes and configurations within a single urban
block. And Roman Ridge Gardens proposes a concrete megastructure where
each apartment stands in its own landscaped space, as if at ground level.

      Elektra House makes especially fruitful connections with
other types of project. The upper floor sits within a larger envelope,
suggesting a building within another building, and this arrangement can
be seen in several of the public projects. It is especially clear in
the positioning of the gallery spaces at the Museum of Contemporary Art
Denver. The external walls of Elektra House are suspended from the edges
of the roof, and the ground-floor space is free of structural supports.
This principle is employed to dramatic effect in the front facade of the
Idea Store Whitechapel and in the cladding of the Corona of the
National Museum of African American History and Culture, which has a
largely unobstructed ground floor because the building's load is taken
by four structural towers. Similarly, the absence of conventional
openings on the street facade of Elektra House renders the scenography
of the building itself the primary visual experience. Adjaye explores
the imaginative potential that comes with breaking the conventional
interior/exterior relationship in many of his public buildings,
differentiating spaces according to their function and enriching
the experience of moving from one position to another. Finally, the
materiality of the house, especially as expressed in the front facade,
suggests a process of assembly in which the components (the plywood
panels, for example) could have been used for another purpose. As in
the later public buildings, the characteristics of a system are put
on display, alongside evidence showing how its components have been
adjusted. Interpreting this evidence is part and parcel of experiencing
Adjaye's buildings.

HILL HOUSE
Port of Spain, Trinidad, 2008-14

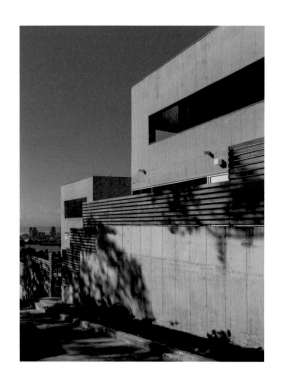

HILL HOUSE
Port of Spain, Trinidad, 2008-14
Side view looking toward the Gulf of Paria

A relief drawing in concrete

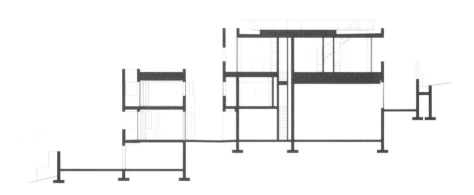

Glass and concrete walls of the main house

Section

NKRON
Ghana, 2008-12

Guest pavilions

Main house addressing landscape

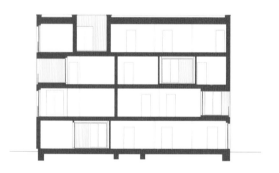

CASE STUDY HOUSING
IBA (International Building Exhibition),
Hamburg, Germany, 2010–13
Exterior view showing loggias

Section

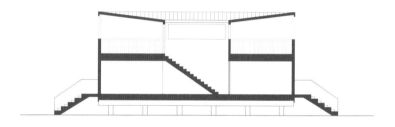

ASEM PA, MAKE IT RIGHT
New Orleans, 2007–11
Exterior view showing raised construction

Section

NANJING HOUSE
Nanjing, China, 2004–12
Exterior view showing stone cladding

Interior view showing suspended
bedroom pods

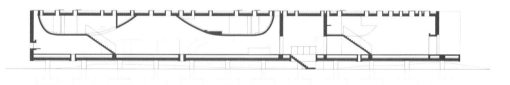

Entrance lobby

Section

SEVEN
New York, 2004–10
Central void

Central court with pool

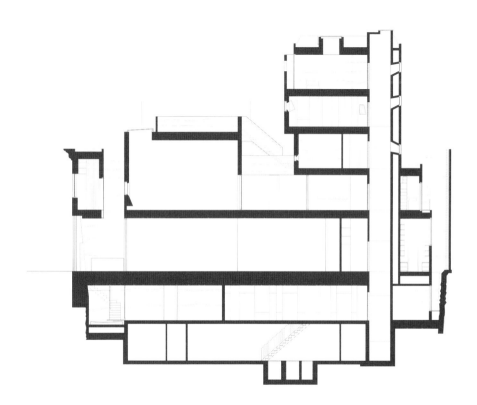

Section

SILVERLIGHT
London, 2002-09
Rear facade

Living space on top floor

Main staircase

LN HOUSE
Denver, Colorado, 2005-07
Street facade

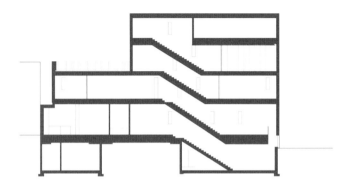

Glazed court

Section

SUNKEN HOUSE
London, 2003-07
Garden facade

View of urban context

Section

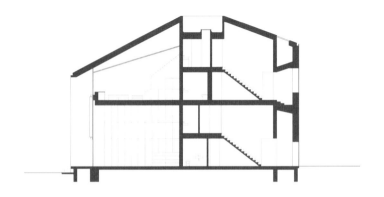

PITCH BLACK
New York, 2003-06
Street view with Pitch Black on left

Section

Rear facade

LOST HOUSE
London, 2002-04
Glazed court

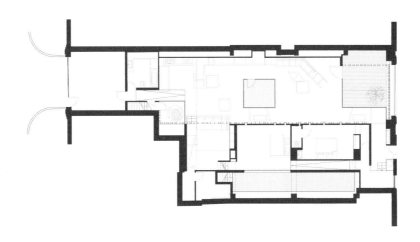

Detail of front facade

Ground-floor plan

DIRTY HOUSE
London, 2001-02
Street facade with anti-graffiti coating

Roof deck

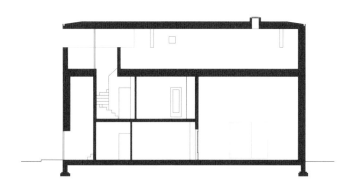

View of studio space

Section

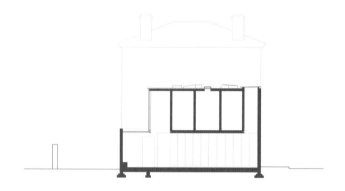

ELEKTRA HOUSE
London, 1998-2000
Street facade

Section

Rear facade

Living space

ROMAN RIDGE GARDENS
Accra, Ghana, designed 2010
View showing beveled balconies,
rendering

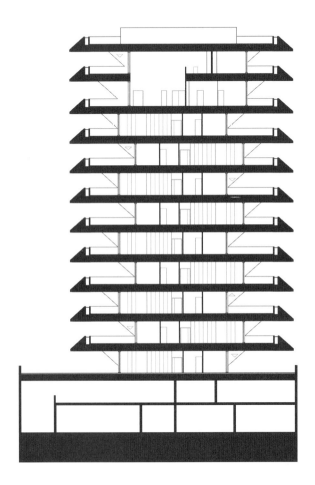

ROMAN RIDGE GARDENS
Accra, Ghana, designed 2010
Section

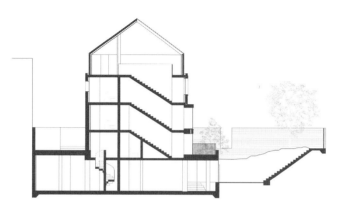

MOLE HOUSE
London, designed 2013
Exterior view showing sunken garden, rendering

Section

HILL HOUSE
Port of Spain, Trinidad, 2008-14
Detail of concrete construction

COSMOPOLITAN PLACE MAKING ANDREA PHILLIPS

(Fig 01) IDEA STORE WHITECHAPEL
London, 2001–05
Café on top floor

(Fig 02) STEPHEN LAWRENCE CENTRE
London, 2004-07
Entrance space

(Fig 03) BERNIE GRANT ARTS CENTRE
London, 2002-07
Entrance space to auditorium building

David Adjaye's public buildings trace a particular set of relations between forms of transnational cosmopolitanism and local civic life. The complexities of these relations fuel his architecture specifically, but they also belong to a much larger circumstance of cosmopolitan representability of which he is very much a part. This entangled and often ambiguous relationship between the life of buildings at the global level and their local use is symptomatic of a phenomenon apparent in urban centers across the world, where histories and patterns of migration and displacement create and sustain the texture of city life. It is also symptomatic of the role of architecture as a form of social production in which the shaping of buildings for local contexts must also be mediated through these same buildings' transnational circulation as object, image, and sign. The Adjaye buildings discussed in this essay exemplify this translocal complex in many ways. Examining them will permit us to unpack how Adjaye approaches what performance theorist Rustom Bharucha has called the "*cosmopolitical* field of economic, social, and political forces" that shape the civic values of his work.[01] Adjaye's designs emerge out of and come to symbolize a desire for cosmopolitan place making, held dear by communities and their cultural leaders, as well as by those who seek to monetize such desire. His buildings provide spaces within which people are able to experience and contemplate new and more transient forms of community belonging, but they are also commissioned for the market value they add to locales. It is this complex, and the way that Adjaye's buildings both defy and contribute to it, that is of significance not simply to those who use the buildings but also to the development of what constitutes civic building.

Although over the past ten years Adjaye has produced an extraordinary range of civic, retail, residential, and master-plan projects across the world, and he is also well known for his collaborative installation work with artists and curators, the examples I will analyze here are all civic buildings in London, the city in which he initially tested many of the ideas that have informed his more recent international projects. This choice is at once pragmatic and strategic. I know these buildings intimately and am imbricated in the artistic and civic culture from which they were developed. But analyzing these London buildings will also shed light on larger questions that inform Adjaye's work—questions regarding the relation between the exquisite nature of objects and materials and the social conditions of neighborhoods and situations; questions about the demand for new cultural spaces and the complex economic, political, and aspirational values from whence the demand comes. There are direct material and sculptural connections in the projects Adjaye has designed since creating these buildings, of course, but also direct relations of cultural, economic, and social use, whether these be with the Francis A. Gregory Library and William O. Lockridge Library, both in Washington, D.C.; the Museum of Contemporary Art Denver in Denver, Colorado; or the National Museum of African American History and Culture (NMAAHC), also in Washington, D.C.

01.   Rustom Bharucha, *Another Asia: Rabindranath Tagore and Okakura Tenshin* (Oxford University Press, 2009), p. 115. [Emphasis added.]

This focus on London thus constitutes the beginning of a reflection on what the legacy of Adjaye's work might be in terms of ideas about community, sociality, and creative production.[02] Out of the patchy and often underfunded picture of local architectural commissioning in the United Kingdom something exceptional emerges; the very porosity of the buildings allows for a form of design use that is not recuperable in terms of gentrification or cultural economics, even as it of course adds significant value to this agenda (in fact, the commissions are often motivated by such hopes).

BERNIE GRANT ARTS CENTRE

The Bernie Grant Arts Centre, opened in 2007 in the Tottenham neighborhood in the north London borough of Haringey, has a midscale multipurpose theater, a number of studio and media spaces, and an enterprise center funded by the Prince's Trust, where young creative entrepreneurs provide "goods or services to public and private sector organisations, community and business groups and individual consumers."[03] (Figs 03 & 04) The building consists of three blocks built on the site of the old council swimming pool: the first, an entrance and visitors' center, is a gray slate steel-framed rectangle built onto the back of the existing protected Victorian facade; the second is the main auditorium, constructed behind the entrance building; the third, the enterprise center, stands behind the auditorium. The main house has a canopy of brown metal slats running diagonally, extending the front of the building and letting shafts of light inside. This simple and generous encasement, angled outward and upward like a canopy at the entrance, provides the complex with its main poetic. The three buildings are surrounded by Edwardian civic architecture—the town hall, a local college, and a fire station—all of which constitute the central hub of Tottenham, arranged on one side of Tottenham Green. The Bernie Grant Arts Centre is busy—its inside messy and disheveled by the comings and goings of local performance groups, its café relaxed, its walls dotted with notices asking for volunteers and posters for upcoming events, its corridors showing signs of use. The theater lobby is dominated by a gray painted concrete structure that serves as a walkway to the upper-floor theater entrance and has seats in its corners—a cumbersome artifact that dissipates the drama of the slatted encasement but provides surprisingly intimate spaces within the beautiful sweep of the building's envelope.

    The Bernie Grant Arts Centre was created to be a catalyst for regeneration in one of the most deprived boroughs in the United Kingdom.[04] Its aim is to "remove barriers to participation in the arts and creative industries [and] celebrate the creativity of a culturally diverse population." As its mission statement puts it,

02.   For example, speaking in 2012 in a video interview on the Washington, D.C., libraries' website about his new neighborhood libraries for the city, Adjaye said, "much of public infrastructure is about paying things, sorting out things, organizing things. Libraries are one of the few parts of public infrastructure which is about the dissemination of knowledge and information for free to the community. It's a very jewel-like part of the public service that's given to any community. For me a library can't just be a simple facility...or utility. It's got to be something that really celebrates this incredible world that is in every page of the book stacks or on the computers that takes people to other places and inspires them. The building has got to be a real cover for this content and not just a soft or subdued version of that. For me the library is a significant hope message of things that are possible." See "William O. Lockridge/Bellevue Library Construction Update," D.C. Public Library, http://dclibrary.org/node/599.

03.   "Enterprise Centre," Bernie Grant Arts Centre, http://www.berniegrantcentre.co.uk/p58.html.

04.   Born in Guyana, Bernie Grant was the Labour Party member of parliament for Haringey from 1987 until his death in 2000. One of the first black MPs in the United Kingdom, Grant is famous for his fight against rate-capping (the imposition of an upper limit on the property tax leviable by a local authority), for his campaign to restore Alexandra Palace, and for his role in the response to the Broadwater Farm Riot in Tottenham in 1985.

(Fig 04) BERNIE GRANT ARTS CENTRE
London, 2002-07
Performance space

The vision of the center as an organisation dedicated to making a substantial contribution to the social and economic regeneration of Tottenham is a key objective of the organisation. We are also committed to being a centre of excellence in the area of training, education and learning, and arts and cultural diversity. We develop projects with partners of regional, national and international significance as well [as] being recognized as of high value locally ... In addition, it is recognized that the creative and cultural sector still largely excludes working class, black, Asian and minority ethnic communities, particularly in positions of power and leadership roles.[05]

This mission, with its mixture of clear ethical premises and creative business aspiration, is now commonplace in the administrative language of urban, publicly funded community organizations. It speaks to the difficult and often compromised conditions in boroughs with historically formed diverse populations struggling to cope with decreased welfare budgets and increased regeneration imperatives. Adjaye's architecture, despite its incredible transnational success, comes from and develops through these scenarios, where questions of spatial and social equality—and the freely expressed and thus classically uneven aesthetics that his architecture produces—meet the economically ambitious techniques of public-private financing and the rhetoric of the cultural industries. At the Bernie Grant Arts Centre, this convergence is expressed in the dark and functional block behind the Edwardian facade as well as the dominant concrete slab at the entrance to the theater that disrupts the sweep of the canopy. In these gestures, the compromises of contemporary civility are made apparent; the desire to encompass diversity and difference set against the well-intentioned managerial culture that clumsily and resignedly embraces entrepreneurialism as a post-welfare state necessity.

STEPHEN LAWRENCE CENTRE

The Stephen Lawrence Centre, [Figs 02 & 05] also opened in 2007, was commissioned with similar aspirations. Located in the old docklands of Deptford in south London, it consists of two buildings connected by a bridge on a site restricted by underground pipework for the public utility Thames Water, as well as by the course of the old River Ravensbourne, a tributary of the Thames, which runs alongside the building and is straddled by two bridges near the center. Adjaye's design echoes these earlier bridges. The relatively large three-floor building is clad in expanded metal mesh and is sharply angled. The facade of the entrance side is made of two panes of glass that sandwich a silver laminate sheet of repeated pattern by the artist Chris Ofili, providing an abstract light motif in the interior when the sun shines through. The smaller cantilevered building contains studios and storage, the larger a suite of media facilities and meeting rooms. The center, which commemorates the life of a black teenager whose ambitions to be an architect were curtailed by his racially motivated murder in a nearby area in 1993, was specifically envisioned to provide social and educational support for young disadvantaged people.[06] Like the Bernie Grant Arts Centre, it does this in part through encouraging enterprise. Symon Sentain, chair of the board of trustees, describes the mission:

05.   "Vision," Bernie Grant Arts Centre, http://www.berniegrantcentre.co.uk/p91.html.

06.   Stephen Lawrence lived in Eltham in southeast London, and was aspiring to be an architect when he was attacked and fatally wounded. The murder caused a national outcry and exposed the community and police protection of the white teenagers who were eventually prosecuted in 2011. A public inquiry into the case, held in 1998 and headed by Sir William MacPherson, accused the police of being "institutionally racist." See "Report of the Stephen Lawrence Inquiry," Sir William MacPherson, Feb. 1999, http://www.archive.official-documents.co.uk/document/cm42/4262/sli-00.htm.

20 years on from Stephen Lawrence's untimely death, we are looking at our future and at how the Trust can continue to be a beacon of inspiration in changing times. There is no doubt that the political, social and economic environment in which the Trust operates is changing. The Government's spending cuts have concentrated the collective mind of the charity sector and sharpened the need to look at different and innovative ways to do business. The Government's localism agenda presents new and different opportunities. With support from a range of partners, we will continue developing the Trust to become a leading sustainable social business, delivering excellent social benefit and change through our service delivery. We can learn from talented people in the business sector and shape our operational approach to maximise its effectiveness and reach. We will build a direct bridge between the young people on our programmes and successful businesses.[07]

Three minutes' walk from Deptford's transport hub, the Stephen Lawrence Centre glistens in the scrubby park that surrounds it. Inside its heavy black doors, the double-height foyer contains a reception desk, a mural, bulletin boards, and a small vitrine containing memorials of Lawrence's life, including his early architectural drawings. A portrait of the young man is perched on an easel, along with various reports and awards won by him, by the Stephen Lawrence Trust (which founded and commissioned the building), and by his mother, Doreen Lawrence, whose battle to have overturned the initial acquittal of his racist murderers is now legendary and who was made a Baroness and entered the House of Lords in 2013. Here too there is information on black and minority ethnic scholarships to various schools of architecture initiated in collaboration with the trust, as well as more general offers of support. The building is quiet at the beginning of the week but fills up toward the end with community groups and training classes.

What is this architectural intervention into the civic, of the civic? How should it be understood as part of a larger and longer narrative of class, race, and opportunity in the city? What are the values of civicness represented in these two buildings, which belong to the top-down funding structures of a welfare state that has disappeared over the course of Adjaye's life? What are the values of civicness represented in the offer of this architecture to be something else, to provide spaces for such questions of civicness differently? If the civic was once incarnated in the stern Victorian and Edwardian buildings of London, like those that stand around the Bernie Grant Arts Centre—the town halls, libraries, hospitals, and galleries, the edifices of a top-down mercantile benevolent structure, built through colonial wealth and dominant into the middle of the twentieth century in the United Kingdom—then how might a new civic emerge from the ruins of this social architecture, a sense of the civic that is embedded in difference, in a flexible and tactical relationship to national and local belonging?

Adjaye's work, suffused with dramatic contrasts and angles and free of fussy ornamentation, is literally embedded in the city, slotted into the workplaces and lives that pass it and use it; it does not rise imperiously into the skyline. In this, his architecture presents a contrast to the still-dominant style. He acknowledges the need for change, particularly in architectural training: "There's a whole patrimonial culture that's been perpetuated by a certain generation, and we've taken it as the norm now, and there's no reason for it. There was a movement in the eighties towards this aggressive, top-down, have-you-been-sanctioned mentality, and we're still in the residue of that as a way of teaching. It's just something that needs to be stopped."[08] He also says of his own architecture, "I'm not interested in these threshold moments where you rise up to enter …We're done with that. I don't want to go up to the temple."[09]

07.   Stephen Lawrence Charitable Trust, http://www.stephenlawrence.org.uk, accessed Dec. 13, 2013.

(Fig 05) STEPHEN LAWRENCE CENTRE
London, 2004-07
Classroom

IDEA STORE WHITECHAPEL

The Idea Store Whitechapel opened in 2005.[Figs 01 & 06] Commissioned by Tower Hamlets Council in London as part of a larger scheme to expand access to further and higher education in the borough, the building is a library as well as an information center, a location for social events, and a cafe. It is remarkable for its colored-glass paneling, recognizable from a distance. Inside, people talk and study, listen to music, and gaze out the windows at the market below. The Whitechapel Market is well established and spreads across the wide pavement, weaving its way into any spare space, inventively arranging and rearranging merchandise, people, and support structures. The market was a key incentive for construction of the building, and Adjaye regularly refers to the importance of market structures in his work. He has built a covered market in Wakefield, West Yorkshire, says that the colors of the Idea Store Whitechapel fascia mimic the colors of the Whitechapel Market awnings, and often discusses the importance of market architectures in Africa in which spaces of trade, community, and conviviality are permeable.

The move to describe libraries as "idea stores," pioneered by the borough of Tower Hamlets is at once a move toward accessibility (on the premise that young people who are unemployed and not participating in formal education and training are alienated by libraries) and an acknowledgement of the capitalization of knowledge production now endemic in Anglo-Saxon pedagogic culture. To the traditional scholar the Idea Store Whitechapel is a noisy and inhospitable place to concentrate; to the first fully digital generation of would-be students the atmosphere is normal and the space allows a freedom, a place to while away some time. The flexibility of knowledge as it emerges in and out of the newly branded library stands in sharp contrast to the increasingly elite university system to which many of the people who use the library have little access.

Saskia Sassen says of Adjaye's work, "these buildings are not simply in public space. They *are* public space (where) discontinuities become an integral part, a component of a space rather than a division between two different spaces articulated as inside/outside, private/public."[10] She describes Adjaye's buildings as spaces in which the complexities of ephemeral and transient engagement negotiate the formal surround of the city, echoing the architect's own desire to open up thresholds, to resist the association of civic building with self-improvement learned through the mimicry of patrimonial ideals. It is thus logical that the Bernie Grant Arts Centre, the Stephen Lawrence Centre, and the Idea Store Whitechapel all struggle to achieve economic fluency and are all marked physically by their years of social use. These are not pristine buildings that are carefully maintained and iconographically policed. It is partly their size and the low level of funding through which they manage to stay open that allows them a certain freedom from signification in the landscape of neoliberalism that otherwise very much dominates London's streets. These are precarious organizations, often one step away from closing, surviving from grant to grant, propelled forward by dedicated but often overstretched staff and exhausted volunteers whose political commitment is hard to sustain in a city of buoyant one-upmanship and rampant privilege. This space is a hard one to maintain—a space of more humble ambitions and community values lodged between political genuflection and assertive demand.

08.   Teresa Fernandez, David Adjaye, Marc McQuade, "Not-obvious," in Marc McQuade, ed., *David Adjaye, Authoring: Re-placing Art and Architecture* (Lars Muller, 2012), p. 110.

09.   Alexandra Lange, "Don't Call David Adjaye a Star-chitect," *New York*, last modified July 15, 2007, http://nymag.com/arts/architecture/features/34729/.

10.   Saskia Sassen, "Built Complexity and Public Engagements," in David Adjaye, Peter Allison, Okwui Enwezor, et al., *Making Public Buildings: Specificity, Customization, Imbrication* (Whitechapel Gallery/Thames and Hudson, 2006), p. 14.

(Fig 06) IDEA STORE WHITECHAPEL
London, 2001-05
Library space

(Fig 07) RIVINGTON PLACE
London, 2003-07
Shared gallery space

How might buildings meet the continued need for spaces of parity and open access, where historic inequalities might be made public and realigned? Adjaye's projects make clear that he is committed to the materiality of such questions. His buildings lack grandeur but are nonetheless imposing, playful, experimental. They produce spaces for people to inhabit without huge fanfare—spaces of social and personal production. It is all the more interesting, therefore, that they have come about at this particular juncture (in the United Kingdom at the very least) of ongoing state withdrawal from the grand narrative of equality, complete with its mundane and ungilded community aesthetic, and its replacement with meritocracy as the guiding principle of city life. These buildings negotiate a path through such a seemingly hostile climate, making architectural statements where there have been none, but doing so at a scale that neither alienates the local built environment or inhibits people's ability to take over the form. The contrast between the ramshackle nature of the buildings' interiors, acquired through use, and their sharp, striking exteriors, is in fact a sign of their success.

RIVINGTON PLACE

As if to demonstrate this paradox between signature building and community use, <u>Rivington Place</u> houses two arts organizations in London's fashionable East End hub, Shoreditch. (Figs 07 & 08) Formed with precast concrete panels and high-gloss steel, and pierced by a grid of deeply recessed windows across eight floors, the structure hosts Iniva (Institute of International Visual Arts) and Autograph ABP (formerly known as the Association of Black Photographers), which both support marginalized and underrepresented artistic and intellectual practices drawing on histories of postcolonial visual art in particular. Iniva was established in 1994 to address an imbalance in the representation of culturally diverse artists, curators, and writers, and it moved to these purpose-built facilities in 2007. The organization creates exhibitions and commissions and supports research and education projects. Autograph ABP was established in 1988 to educate the public about photography, cultural diversity, and human rights. Both organizations are funded by the Arts Council of England and both attest to the complex and irregular history of the British art establishment's relationship with issues of cultural representation and the practices of artists whose ethnic and social backgrounds identify them as minority.

Stuart Hall, a founding chair of Iniva's board of trustees and a key voice in the demand for an arts institution in the United Kingdom that addresses its fraught but historically significant cosmopolitan culture, writes of Adjaye's work that it "draws on the diverse influences of a variety of global architectural worlds. This is a hybrid, nomadic, diasporic architecture, shaped and de-centered by a short lifetime of negotiating between different cultures." Describing Adjaye's houses but equally applicable to his civic buildings, and citing the architect's childhood in Tanzania and his teenage years in north London, Hall continues,

> Whilst being thoroughly steeped in and at home with modern Western architecture, constantly remaking and tampering with Modernism's essential clean line and white cube, Adjaye has studiously evaded any overarching grand narrative, eschewing the search for that singular mastery of structure and function which characterized so much of architectural Modernism. Assimilationist and anti-foundational by temper, committed to the more fragmentary character of modern urban life—the fluid, diverse, inclusive, flexible, multi-use, contradictory, transparent is where his houses are most at home.[11]

11. Stuart Hall, "Negotiating Architecture," in David Adjaye, *Houses: Recycling, Reconfiguring, Rebuilding*, ed. Peter Allison (Thames and Hudson, 2005), p. 10.

(Fig 08) RIVINGTON PLACE
London, 2003-07
Stuart Hall Library

Hall's understanding of Adjaye's work as both assimilationist and anti-foundational describes not simply the structure but the atmosphere of the London buildings described here. Postcolonial theorist Leela Gandhi, writing about what she terms "affective" rather than historically sited communities, suggests that colonial fantasies of antagonism between ethnicities, powers, and nations are based on a "craving for the hygiene of oppositionality" that might fend off the "psychic contagion" of cosmopolitanism as it exists on pragmatic and subjective grounds. Gandhi instead asserts the value of "an inchoate, provisional and incoherent form of politics that might show society its wealth of affectional possibility."[12] Adjaye's buildings exude such "psychic contagion." They provide space within which people can imagine new forms of citizenship, as well as struggle with the frameworks of existing antagonistic structures.

As proliferating urban building fills all the spaces where people can just be, as every scrap of land is once again colonized for profit, Adjaye's interventions eschew the kind of civility that you can buy, that can be accessed only by those with enough money, cultural privilege, or entitlement. Simply put, his buildings are not about power. Of course Adjaye does not only build this type of project, made of relatively cheap materials and at a relatively small scale; he has also built many much larger projects as well as the private houses and artistic collaborations for which he is perhaps best known. But we can learn a lot from these building types about the humility of attempts to cross the divide between public and private, top-down and bottom-up politics. What Adjaye's buildings do is call for—and exemplify—a type of civicness that attempts to mix political and affective zones together, thus allowing those that use them to perform their relation to the city and the neighborhood in ways that are "cosmopolitical" at informal, often unnoticed, scales, in ways that repurpose what we understand as public (in the sense that publicness is divested of its heavily regulated connotations). These civic buildings suggest a more complex and nuanced account of the inhabitance of the city, of the market, of social and communal space. In them, the civic loses its spatial and temporal, generational and class-based framework and instead acquires an openness to more composite and politically intricate ways of living together.

12.   Leela Gandhi, *Affective Communities: Anticolonial Thought, Fin-de-Siecle Radicalism, and the Politics of Friendship* (Duke University Press, 2006), p. 185.

DEMOC
KNOW

ACY OF
LEDGE

WILLIAM O. LOCKRIDGE LIBRARY
Washington, D.C., 2008–12
Exterior view showing detached pavilions

If some of David Adjaye's houses are inward-looking and undemonstrative in appearance, the projects in this section are open and inviting. Many of them appear to float above a transparent ground floor, showing how the building is accessed. This was not possible at the Nobel Peace Center, where instead a freestanding arch directs visitors to the entrance. This motif is repeated in the canopy of the auditorium building at the Bernie Grant Arts Centre and in the two-hundred-foot long porch on the south facade of the National Museum of African American History and Culture. In the two Idea Stores, as well as later buildings, the front facades are canted to address the directions from which people will approach, and they set up wedge-shaped spaces inside the buildings that encourage movement in and out. These measures are, however, part of a larger strategy to suggest the purpose of the building in its external silhouette, whereas discerning the details of the program requires exploration of the interior. For this reason, Adjaye's buildings are especially porous, often with several entrances, multiple circulation routes, and a variety of destinations. As in a film, the journey may involve surprising turns, shady passages followed by moments of illumination, broad vistas, and points of return. Within a highly calculated structure that employs advanced energy technologies, complex cladding systems, and modern communications systems, practical considerations are closely overlaid by an equally orchestrated experience of light, texture, and space.

In the analytical process that underpins his designs, Adjaye draws on his African heritage. Returning to the continent as an architect, he could see that buildings he had known since childhood had been conceived by Western modernists complete with devices that address the harsh climate and the local culture, such as deeply shaded volumes and sunbreak screens. He refers to such buildings as examples of "tropical modernism" and has broadened this category to include any building that embraces modern concepts and technologies and, at the same time, takes identifiable steps to engage with local conditions and circumstances. He explored this theme in radio interviews with Indian architect Charles Correa and the late Brazilian architect Oscar Niemeyer. A second insight concerns what Adjaye terms "African abstraction" as represented in the creative arts of the continent. He sees the forms and patterns of African artifacts, compared with the classical tradition in the West, as a resource for navigating the complexity of the contemporary world. The consequences for his work have been far-reaching. Studying tropical modernism revealed to Adjaye how the gap between a set of abstract principles—the systems embodied in contemporary technology, for instance—and local circumstances provides an opportunity for a unique synthesis that reconciles divergent objectives on a poetic basis. Identifying this gap and how it might be bridged is the key move in Adjaye's work. When the first generation of his public buildings was published, he put his cards on the table by including with each project a relevant example of African abstraction to illustrate the source of the poetic synthesis he had in mind. This was a manifesto moment, suggesting that tropical modernism had come full circle and returned to Europe. Since then Adjaye has continued to develop his methodology, with a broader range of poetic references.

WILLIAM O. LOCKRIDGE LIBRARY
Washington, D.C., 2008–12
Exterior view showing protected entrance

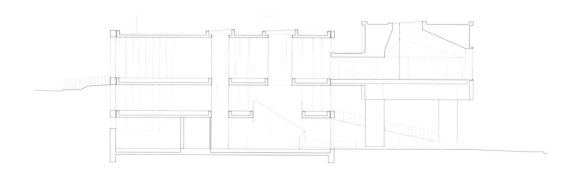

WILLIAM O. LOCKRIDGE LIBRARY
Washington, D.C., 2008–12
Computer space

Section

Teen services space

View of staircase on ground floor

FRANCIS A.GREGORY LIBRARY
Washington, D.C., 2008–12
Front facade

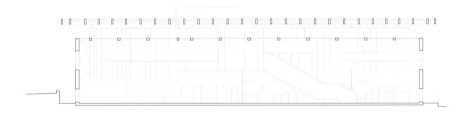

Section

WAKEFIELD MARKET HALL
Wakefield, United Kingdom, 2005-08
View of covered market

Section through covered
and enclosed market halls

MUSEUM OF CONTEMPORARY ART DENVER
Denver, Colorado, 2004-07
Front facade

View of gallery space

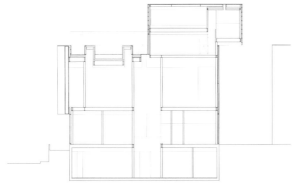

Section

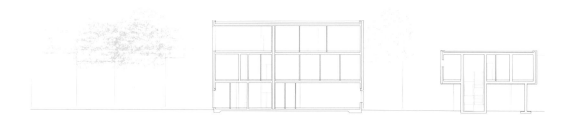

STEPHEN LAWRENCE CENTRE
London, 2004-07
View of exterior

Section

Roof deck

RIVINGTON PLACE
London, 2003-07
Street view

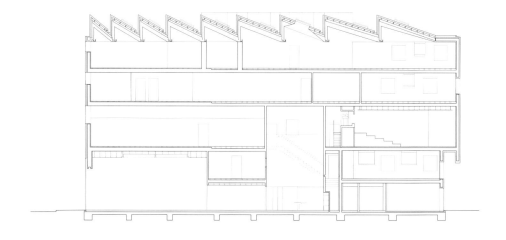

Three-story lobby

Section

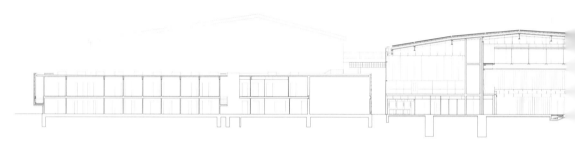

BERNIE GRANT ARTS CENTRE
London, 2002—07
Front facade of auditorium building

Site section showing (right to left) gateway,
auditorium, and enterprise buildings

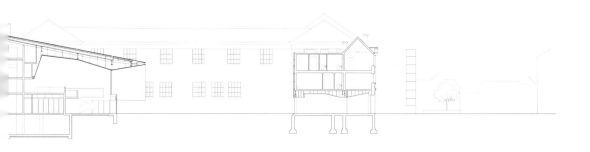

IDEA STORE WHITECHAPEL
London, 2001–05
Street view

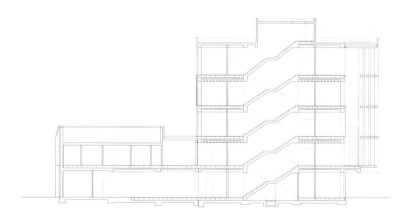

Dance studio

Section

IDEA STORE CHRISP STREET
London, 2002-04
Front facade

View of main library space

NOBEL PEACE CENTER
Oslo, Norway, 2002–05
Freestanding entrance canopy

The Nobel Field

Democracy of Knowledge

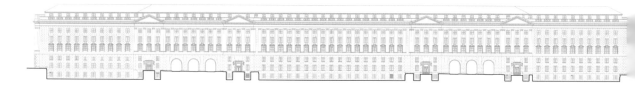

NATIONAL MUSEUM OF
AFRICAN AMERICAN HISTORY AND CULTURE
Washington, D.C., 2009-16
North-south section with the Washington Monument

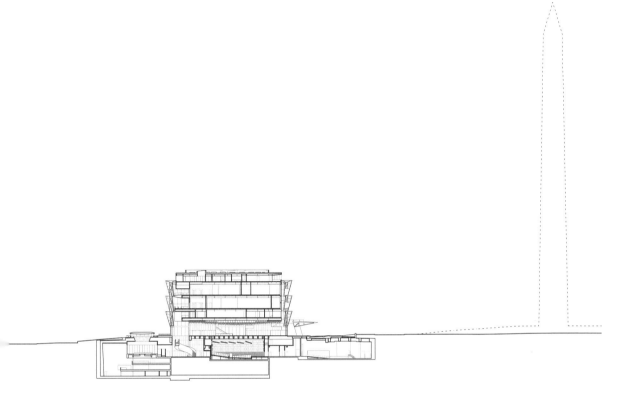

NATIONAL MUSEUM OF
AFRICAN AMERICAN HISTORY AND CULTURE
Washington, D.C., 2009-16

View from the National Mall showing
the South Porch, rendering

NATIONAL MUSEUM OF
AFRICAN AMERICAN HISTORY AND CULTURE
Washington, D.C., 2009–16
Construction view

MEMO—MASS EXTINCTION MEMORIAL OBSERVATORY
Portland, United Kingdom, designed 2009
View showing clifftop location, rendering

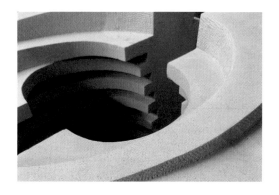

Interior view showing spiral ramp, rendering

Detail of model

CAPE COAST SLAVERY MUSEUM
Cape Coast, Ghana, designed 2012
Exterior view showing raised volume and
lens windows, rendering

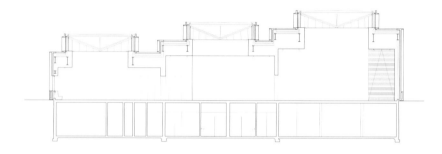

COLGATE CENTER FOR ART AND CULTURE
Colgate University, Hamilton, New York, designed 2014
Aerial view showing (front to back)
Picker, Longyear, and community buildings, model

Section

MUSEUM OF HISTORY, ARTS AND CULTURE
Loango, Republic of the Congo, designed 2014
Exterior view showing light scoops,
rendering

VARANASI SILKWEAVING FACILITY
Varanasi, India, designed 2013
Exterior view looking across the
River Ganges, rendering

Community space, rendering

Weaving hall, rendering

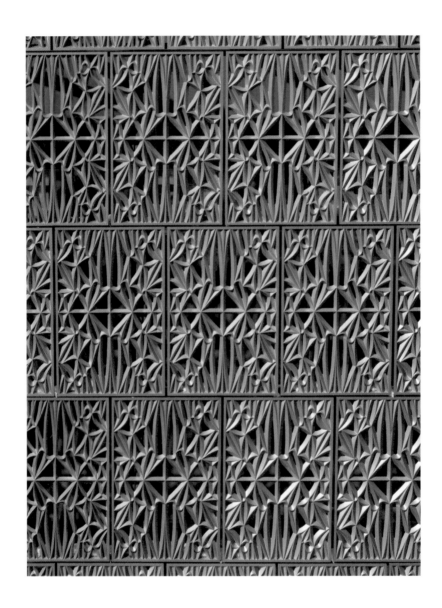

NATIONAL MUSEUM OF
AFRICAN AMERICAN HISTORY AND CULTURE
Washington, D.C., 2009–16
Detail of prototype facade

GESTURES OF
AFFILIATION
OKWUI ENWEZOR

(Fig 01) DIRTY HOUSE
London, 2001-02
Detail of street facade

(Fig 02) ELEKTRA HOUSE
London, 1998-2000
Front facade, street view

I have settled on the image of ships in motion across the spaces between Europe, America, Africa, and the Caribbean as a central organizing symbol for this enterprise and as my starting point. The image of the ship—a living, microcultural, micro-political system in motion—is especially important for historical and theoretical reasons…. Ships immediately focus attention on the middle passage, on the various projects for redemptive return to an African homeland, on the circulation of ideas and activists, as well as the movement of key cultural and political artefacts: tracts, books, gramophone records, and choirs.

Paul Gilroy, *The Black Atlantic: Modernity and Double Consciousness*

At the end of daybreak, this town sprawled-flat …
And in this inert town, this squalling throng so astonishingly
detoured from its cry as this town has been
from its movement, from its meaning,
not even worried, detoured from its true cry,
the only cry you would have wanted to hear because
you feel it alone belongs to this town;
because you feel it lives in it in some deep refuge
and pride in this inert town, this throng detoured
from its cry of hunger, of poverty, of revolt, of hatred,
this throng so strangely chattering and mute.

Aimé Césaire, *Notebook of a Return to the Nativeland*

ON POSTCOLONIAL REALISM

Since founding his firm in 2000, David Adjaye has made an inexorable and visible shift in the language and philosophy of his architectural vision. As his practice has advanced to larger and more complex projects across several continents, so has the conceptual impetus to address important historical questions that have to do with social, political, and cultural issues that attach to architecture's metropolitan contexts. In the process Adjaye has had to clarify how aesthetic references derived especially from the meshing of modern architectural discourse and the idioms of African abstraction can infuse the formal and material language of his buildings with new vitality. Today Adjaye's designs encompass domestic, civic, and commercial structures, as well as experimental commissions that fuse art and architecture. His practice extends to the creation of master plans, urbanism, furniture design, and teaching. Of particular note is African Metropolitan Architecture, an eleven-year-long research project to map the urban and architectural heritage of every capital city in Africa.[01] This vast, ongoing, and unprecedented endeavor presents a rich terrain of analytical possibility and a fruitful resource for understanding how the effects of modernism, colonialism, and postcolonialism, as well as the ideologies of nation building and modernization, have shaped African urban forms.[02]

01.   Due to the exigencies of conflict, Mogadishu, Somalia, and Juba, South Sudan, have yet to be studied.

02.   For a comprehensive overview of this research, see David Adjaye and Peter Allison, *African Metropolitan Architecture* (Rizzoli, 2011), also published as *Adjaye, Africa, Architecture: A Photographic Survey of Metropolitan Architecture* (Thames and Hudson, 2011).

More than any architect working today, Adjaye's practice is deeply inscribed in the spaces of postcolonial realism. Such realism abjures what the philosopher V. Y. Mudimbe refers to as "ethnological reason" in order to "imagine the possibility of a reversal of anthropology's perspective" by employing *logique métisse* (mestizo logic).[03] What may be the possible effects of Adjaye's work at this historical moment? As a young African practicing in a field dominated by older Europeans and Asians, Adjaye, like his colleagues from Iran, India, China, the Middle East, and other non-European locales, represents a shift in global networks of knowledge and the emergence of experts who defy traditional hegemonic structures of cultural capital. His work brings a needed African postcolonial and cosmopolitan voice into the discourse of contemporary architecture. Especially as African economies continue to expand at robust rates, the need for new infrastructural investments in the continent is also growing (just as happened in China fifteen years ago). Add to this the desire of African business, cultural, political, and intellectual leaders to rewrite the negative narratives that have consistently dismissed Africa and Africans as serious partners in the dialogue of modernization, and we have a clearer picture of the space in which Adjaye is currently working.

His practice has evolved organically, from making robust and sublime domestic buildings (often located in multicultural, cosmopolitan urban contexts) to producing larger buildings that aim to democratize the experience of public architecture and acknowledge the heterogeneity of contemporary urban identities. Adjaye's early projects were marked by their modesty, intimacy, and privacy. Each of these attributes was explored in relation to precision of scale, rigor of form, and integrity of material. Although the early commissions were, as domestic architecture, scaled for everyday living, because of their location in ethnically and economically mixed neighborhoods they required different kinds of architectural speculation to effectively situate their strong physicality and materiality within the existing cultural and social fabric.

A number of the domestic buildings, such as London's Dirty House (Fig 01) and Elektra House (Fig 02) were testing grounds for Adjaye's sculptural approach. Their solid forms have the scale and presence of small monuments and an unmistakable but enigmatic visual clarity that sets them apart from their surroundings. One can, for example, stand in front of Elektra House yet completely miss it. The house is all too visible; quietly withdrawn yet present in its location. Perhaps it can be overlooked because of pedestrians' expectations that a house will have a door and some windows facing the street, whereas Elektra House is a structure-cum-object with no door and no windows on this frontage—just a blank facade of darkened plywood panels that make it look boarded up. The structure (a kind of wooden Kaaba) resembles a sculpture more than a building for domestic living. To conjure such a form in a working class neighborhood of utilitarian brick houses was a bold thought experiment; it seems that Adjaye wanted to manifest an uncompromising directness and refusal of the quotidian. Making a plain, unadorned facade the central defining feature of Elektra House certainly accomplished this.

These domestic projects brought early critical notice to Adjaye's refined yet rough-hewn architectural language. But over the last decade his public and civic buildings' spirited response to their context and to cultural and political change have opened further opportunities, particularly in the rich cosmopolitan culture of places like London. Thinking of the composition of communities in London or New York inevitably brings up the issue of social space. As Henri

03.   V. Y. Mudimbe, *The Idea of Africa* (Indiana University Press/James Currey, 1994). For further insight into Mudimbe's exploration of the idea of mixing, syncretism, and hybridity, see ibid., pp. 38-70. Jean-Loup Amselle coined the term *logique métisse*; see Amselle, *Logique métisses: Anthropologie de l'identité en Afrique et ailleurs*, Bibliothèque scientifique Payot (Payot, 1990).

Lefebvre taught us, the production of social space operates on a number of levels that are imbued with mental, physical, and symbolic attributes.[04] Crafting architecture in the spatially mobile conditions of contemporary cities is a different endeavor than doing so in largely monocultural contexts. Addressing mixed communities with mixed cultural legacies certainly prizes open doors into the burgeoning transnational social sphere. How do today's global cities and the shift to virtual space and digital communities produced by new technologies—and their open-ended conceptions of space—challenge modernist expectations of unitary forms of architecture? Similarly, how does the current climate encourage the development of aesthetically modular, recalcitrant, and complex designs? Architecture has only barely begun rethinking its relationship to the migrant identities and subjectivities of global cities in the way that late-nineteenth-century designs for workers' housing and twentieth-century public housing schemes did. Perhaps, in mixed communities of Muslims and non-Muslims, Hindus and Christians, atheists and believers, rich and poor, global urban architecture has to rethink its inherited traditions.

Adjaye has attended to these issues through nuanced representational design references. All of his work is grounded in a clear recognition of the interplay of the legacies of modernity and secularism in shaping living arrangements in modern cities. Included in these legacies are the histories of migration, the struggle for housing reform to accommodate the needs of migrants, and often the incorporation of new iconographies within postcolonial communities.[05] A number of his important public buildings have been remarkable, low-key civic structures whose central attributes emerge from the secular tradition of the democratic public sphere, which extends today to encompass the contemporary demands of civil society, civil rights, and democratic politics: the Nobel Peace Center, Oslo, Norway; the Idea Store Whitechapel and Idea Store Chrisp Street, both in the East End of London; the Bernie Grant Arts Centre, London; the Stephen Lawrence Centre, London; Rivington Place, London; and the more recent Francis A. Gregory Library and William O. Lockridge Library, both in Washington, D.C.[06] These buildings constitute exercises in thinking the civic and inclusive function of architecture within global multicultural and transnational movements.

Significantly, with the libraries, Adjaye imagined elegant buildings that do not condescend to the community or the users of the spaces. He was careful to make rigorous, high-quality contemporary buildings but rejected complicated and overproduced designs that elevated iconicity over substance, or that aggrandized him as the creator but confounded, alienated, or excluded the users. Rather, he approached the design of these buildings with an eye toward integrating the structures into the socioeconomic and politico-cultural patterns of the municipal landscape and into the ongoing activities surrounding the buildings. For example, by eschewing a substantial setback from its busy sidewalk, the Idea Store Whitechapel seamlessly bridges the marketplace of

04.   See Henri Lefebvre, *The Production of Space*, trans. Donald Nicholson-Smith (Blackwell Publishing, 1991).

05.   Born in Tanzania to Ghanaian parents, Adjaye grew up during the turbulent early decades of African decolonization and independence movements. His parents were members of the pioneer generation of postcolonial Africans and, due to his father's job as a diplomat, the family moved to Egypt, Lebanon, and Saudi Arabia before finally settling in London in the late 1970s, just as British cities were being convulsed by urban riots and clashes between immigrants and the police. It might be useful in this sense to speculate on what effects (or lack thereof) Adjaye's own experience of migration has had on his architecture.

06.   The writings of Jürgen Habermas on the question and evolution of the public sphere in Europe have been very influential, especially in its political, social, institutional, and civic elaboration. The congeries of private demands on public forms of representation and representability strongly affect how we may address the locus of civic architecture. See Jürgen Habermas, *The Structural Transformation of the Public Sphere: An Inquiry into the Category of Bourgeois Society*, trans. Thomas Burger (Polity Press, 1992).

commodities, represented by the bustling street-trading activities and lean-to shops, and that of knowledge and ideas, each of which exploits specific types of economic and social capital. (Fig 03) This is a Lefebvrean disguise par excellence, in the sense that the building positions itself between a mental space (a place of refuge and thinking) and a real space (a socially and economically vibrant street culture). It is as if the grammar of everyday life doubles itself into the folds of contemplative and subjective life. In so doing, designs such as the Idea Stores not only successfully explore the fundamental alignment between the civic and public situations produced by migrant experiences and the rich cultural contributions they make to London, they also brilliantly assert Adjaye's design language within the politics of form.

DIALECTICS OF CIVIC ARCHITECTURE

Although most critical writing on his practice has not taken full account of this, Adjaye's work is materially and conceptually dialectical. His buildings are also, especially in recent commissions, highly symbolic and dialogical propositions. Rather than grand statements or self-regarding creations, Adjaye's designs are made for and conceived around the core values of *res publica*, the commonwealth, and therefore as places to experience the democracy of knowledge. Moreover, especially in the case of buildings crafted in response to specific social demographics (Asian and African immigrants in east London, a primarily African American neighborhood in Washington, D.C.), his projects become, to borrow sociologist and philosopher Maurizio Lazzarato's phrase, centers for the production of subjectivity.[07]

The remainder of this essay will focus on three public buildings that respond to the necessity to inscribe new types of historical content into architecture itself: the National Museum of African American History and Culture (NMAAHC), in Washington, D.C.; the Cape Coast Slavery Museum in Cape Coast, Ghana; and the Stephen Lawrence Centre. Each commemorates and responds to a desire to explore and script global multicultural and transnational experiences. These buildings may be approached as "gestures of affiliation": modes of belonging that reconceive the scattered trajectories of migrant lives and selves within seemingly monolithic cultural landscapes. More importantly, the structures transparently manifest Adjaye's dialectical and dialogical architectural vision. The occasions for these buildings are the histories of African slavery, exile, and migration. They are about narratives of black lives and experiences in the global sphere. Or, as the eminent African American writer, political activist, cultural critic, and Pan-Africanist W. E. B. Du Bois put it in the title of his classic 1903 book, they are about *The Souls of Black Folk*.[08]

These three buildings share one feature: they address the renewal of historical exploration of African memories, from the scattered trajectories of exile, enslavement, and—to quote Paul Gilroy again—the "projects for redemptive return to an African homeland." Such redemptive return obviously is based more on spiritual conceptions of cultural heritage and imaginative travel, on a desire to forge shared links, the reiteration of what remains of tenuous bonds, than of actual physical return. In other words, Adjaye's recent forays into architecture are an occasion for scripting the text of social memorialization, and they thus touch on how the making of memory and the construction of spaces bear on the relationship between the sacred and the secular, the

07.   Maurizio Lazzarato, *Signs and Machines: Capitalism and the Production of Subjectivity* (Semiotext(e), 2014).

08.   W. E. B. Dubois, *The Souls of Black Folk* (A. C. McClurg, 1903).

(Fig 03) IDEA STORE WHITECHAPEL
London, 2001-05
Street view with market stalls on right

public and the civic. The social production of memory requires texts, symbols, and spaces, for it is within these inscriptions that the purpose of the museum as a site of commemoration becomes sharply illuminated.

Lefebvre identified three forces in the production of space:

1. *Spatial practice*, which embraces production and reproduction and the particular locations and spatial sets characteristic of each social formation. Spatial practice ensures continuity and some degree of cohesion. In terms of social space, and of each member of a given society's relationship to that space, this cohesion implies a guaranteed level of competence and a specific level of performance.

2. *Representations of space*, which are tied to the relations of production and to the "order" which those relations impose, and hence to knowledge, to signs, to codes, and to frontal "relations."

3. *Representational spaces*, embodying complex symbolisms, sometimes coded, sometimes not, linked to the clandestine or underground side of social life, as also to art (which may come eventually to be defined less as a code of space than as a code of representational spaces).[09]

This "conceptual triad" may in fact describe the dialectics of civic architecture. In particular, the architecture of museums designed to display artifacts documenting violence, displacement, and injustice demands not only new codes of space, but also new codes of representational spaces. It calls for, in addition to logics of building, logics of dwelling and thinking, to echo the title of Heidegger's classic essay.[10] We might say that these spaces, by being repositories for diverse cultural artifacts, have to account for the production of the archive, the practice of commemoration, and relations of consecration. That is, how do cultures remember, commemorate, honor, and narrate their history, past, and aspirations?

These questions are central to the ways in which the NMAAHC and the Cape Coast Slavery Museum spaces will come to embody both the sacral principles of the shrine and the secular ambitions from which logics of civic identity are constituted. In this sense, the spatial practice of the National Mall in Washington, D.C., symbolizes the ground zero where America's lofty self-image and its actual checkered past have been neatly joined. For over two hundred years, the Mall has been a gathering place and the resolute (at times, too resolute) mechanism for embedding the evolving memories and accounts of the American republic in the nation's dramatization of its founding principles. The lack of strong visual acknowledgment of slavery and the enslaved within America's gallery of monuments and memorials has been a stain on the nation's image of itself. According to its official website:

09.   Lefebvre, *The Production of Space*, p. 33.

10.   An important touchstone for architecture—and a classic philosophical work around which Lefebvre's conceptual triad is aligned—is, of course, Heidegger's seminal 1951 essay "Building, Dwelling, Thinking," in *Poetry, Language, Thought*, trans. Albert Hofstadter (Harper and Row, 1971), pp. 145–61. Jacques Derrida's notion of domiciliation in relation to his theory of the archive brings further insight into the concept, which he connects to the Greek origin of the term *archive*: "As is the case for the Latin *archivum* or *archium* (a word that is used in the singular as was the French archive, formerly employed as a masculine singular: un archive), the meaning of "archive," its only meaning, comes to it from the Greek *arkheion*: initially a house, a domicile, an address, the residence of the superior magistrates, the archons, those who commanded...On account of their publicly recognized authority, it is at their home, in that place which is their house (private house, family house, or employee's house), that official documents are filed...It is thus, in this domiciliation, in this house arrest, that archives take place." See Derrida, *Archive Fever: A Freudian Impression*, trans. Eric Prenowitz (University of Chicago Press, 1996), p. 2.

[Its] origins are as old as the capital city itself. The open spaces and parklands envisioned by Pierre L'Enfant's plan, which was commissioned by President George Washington, created an ideal stage for national expressions of remembrance, observance, celebration, and expression of First Amendment rights. With everything from colossal monuments to commemorative gardens, from presidential inaugurals to civil rights demonstrations, NAMA [the National Mall and Memorial Parks] hosts history in the making. Numerous First Amendment activities and special events are held in the park each year. The park continues to evolve as Americans seek new ways to recognize our heritage.[11]

Set in this heavily symbolic and ideological public space where the American nation comes to recognize, remember, and celebrate (namely archive, commemorate, and consecrate) its textured history is Adjaye's NMAAHC, whose three-tiered structure was inspired by the geometric three-tiered crown surmounting the elaborate figurative veranda posts carved by the Yoruba sculptor Olowe of Ise at the turn of the twentieth century (see p. 69). Adjaye Associates' summary of the design concept states: "The design rests on three cornerstones: the 'corona' shape and form of the building; the extension of the building out into the landscape—the porch; and the bronze filigree envelope."[12] This is a building that powerfully foregrounds "codes of representational spaces," expressing formally what Lefebvre's conceptual triad describes analytically. And it elucidates the relations of social production that connect the spatial concepts of the archive, the mnemonic registers of commemoration, and the symbolic codes of consecration.

Although Adjaye's museum is neither a memorial nor a monument, its very construction unmistakably evokes these two increasingly controversial entities. Art historian Mark Godfrey has written persuasively on the difficulties and challenges posed by the making of monuments and memorials.[13] Similar controversies have bedeviled important works of architectural memory such as Daniel Liebeskind's Jewish Museum in Berlin. It is important to bear in mind that memorials and monuments, rather than simply being devices to make memory, history, or structures of remembering, are fundamentally representational spaces designed to explore ruptures in memory, opacities of history, and fractures in remembering. Especially since no monument or memorial referencing slavery has ever been constructed in the gallery of American monuments and memorials that includes the Washington Monument, Thomas Jefferson Memorial, Lincoln Memorial, Franklin Delano Roosevelt Memorial, D.C. War Memorial, World War II Memorial, Korean War Veterans Memorial, Vietnam Veterans Memorial, and George Mason Memorial, Adjaye's museum takes on even greater significance—and a bigger burden. It must be both a secular space responding to the traditions of American democracy and a sacral space corresponding to African American yearning to belong to the republic.(Figs 04 & 05)

The NMAAHC will join the monuments and memorials on the National Mall, the same hallowed national space that for centuries has excluded African memories. The question of African memories is fundamental. It is in exploring their social and historical meaning that a second question can be raised: what other relationship to Africa beyond the symbolic or structural can

---

11.　"National Mall & Memorial Parks," last modified June 18, 2014, http://www.nps.gov/nama/historyculture/index.htm.

12.　For a description of the building see "Smithsonian NMAAHC," http://www.adjaye.com/projects/civic-buildings/smithsonian-national-museum-of-african-american-history-and-culture-nmaahc/.

13.　Mark Godfrey, *Abstraction and the Holocaust* (Yale University Press, 2007).

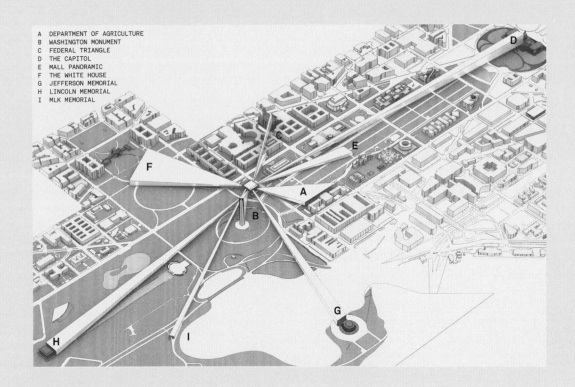

A DEPARTMENT OF AGRICULTURE
B WASHINGTON MONUMENT
C FEDERAL TRIANGLE
D THE CAPITOL
E MALL PANORAMIC
F THE WHITE HOUSE
G JEFFERSON MEMORIAL
H LINCOLN MEMORIAL
I MLK MEMORIAL

(Fig 04) NATIONAL MUSEUM OF AFRICAN
AMERICAN HISTORY AND CULTURE
Washington, D.C., 2009–16
Schematic view showing position on the National Mall

design inscribe in relation to the mnemonic? The complexity required to negotiate and navigate the sensitive history of slavery brings forth as well the continent's relationship to that history. To examine this point one must look past the monumental museum rising on the Washington Mall and cast eyes toward the African coast, to the Cape Coast Slavery Museum in Cape Coast, Ghana.(Figs 07 & 10) Between the sixteenth and nineteenth centuries, the trade in Africans flourished, sending millions of men and women (the majority from West Africa and a sizeable number from Central Africa) to Europe, North and South America, and the Caribbean. The trauma of the Triangular Trade and the harrowing Middle Passage has had enduring social consequences and has vividly stamped the cultural identity of the New World, where millions of slaves were taken. The Middle Passage has been an important leitmotif in this narrative, in the search for the broken links among diasporic Africans, Africa, Europe, and the Americas.

It is in reflection of that search and the complex narratives accompanying and surrounding it that Adjaye's Cape Coast Slavery Museum is now being planned. The building is designed specifically to commemorate and inscribe Africa's participation in the Triangular Trade. In the museum's narrative, Africans are no longer treated solely as victims, but also as active agents in the catastrophe. Without eliding the complicity of African warrant chiefs and merchant elites in the trade, the museum will also present the vital link between Africa and peoples of African descent in Europe and the Americas to explore paths of understanding and reconciliation. The Cape Coast Slavery Museum will rise on one side adjacent to Cape Coast Castle, a slave fortress, one of the more than 140 that dot the continent's coast, and from which millions of Africans were shipped to the New World.(Fig 06) Adjaye's design imagines a dialogue between the ancient fortress and the new structure, delineated by an expansive ocher-colored esplanade that connects the two buildings and then leads down to the beach and stretches away to the sea. The challenge facing Adjaye in designing these two museum projects in Washington, D.C., and Cape Coast is how to reimagine the absence of commemorative structures that give physical sanctuary to the experiences, and how to incorporate the mnemonic expectations that will shadow the museums in the years to come. The Cape Coast Slavery Museum and the NMAAHC should be understood as two sides of one coin. The intersection of two narratives, as well as specific microhistories belonging to each national context, offers Adjaye the rare opportunity to construct a unique architectural object for each site.

In the United States such buildings commemorating the memories of African slaves and the contributions of their descendants to the making of the American republic have been desired, debated, and lobbied for since the Emancipation Proclamation was issued and the Civil War ended. One unsatisfactory result was the Emancipation Monument, also known as the Freedman's Memorial to Abraham Lincoln, located near the site of the NMAAHC in Lincoln Park in the Capitol Hill neighborhood of Washington, D.C.(Fig 08) This bronze figurative sculpture by Thomas Ball depicts Lincoln, formally clothed in suit and tie, standing with his right hand on a rounded lectern, while his left hand waves gracefully, as if blessing the crouched figure of an African man kneeling at his feet, with broken chains signifying the loosing of the bonds of slavery. This representation was very controversial at the time of its design because, although it purportedly commemorates the freeing of the slaves, it still depicts the African figure as inferior to his supposed liberator. Representations of slavery in American culture have been both uneven and fraught with disagreements. The recent Oscar-winning film *12 Years a Slave* (2013) by the British director Steve McQueen magisterially explores and examines the representations of bondage and freedom.[14]

(Fig 05) NATIONAL MUSEUM OF
AFRICAN AMERICAN HISTORY AND CULTURE
Washington, D.C., 2009-16
Aerial view showing the museum to the
right of the Washington Monument

MUSEAL [15]

Perhaps we should turn from the specific politics of representation, commemoration, and memorialization to inquire into the possible narratives that might come to the fore in the process of "musealizing" African memories. The epigraph from Paul Gilroy with which this essay begins offers a powerful image of the triangulation of Africa, Europe, and the Americas in the making of New World African identities. The term he uses for this triangulation is "double consciousness," a concept borrowed from Du Bois, who had coined it to describe the historical experience of diasporic Africans in the Americas in a situation of active ongoing negotiation, absorption, and transculturation, by African Americans, of European and African cultures. This interaction, from the slave narrative to Negro spirituals and blues to jazz, contains elements of African and European forms and produced the hyphenated cultural identity of black peoples of the New World, and with that a "double consciousness." Gilroy examines this idea by analyzing closely the literary, sonic, and political productions of diasporic Africans. The cultural and political maps he posits of the "Black Atlantic," which encompasses Europe, the Americas, and the Caribbean, emerge powerfully through his reading of the transitions of the Middle Passage, which in turn testifies to the historical awareness of the specters of slavery and how much it is bound up with the history of modernity and its multiple discontents. The ship in motion, ploughing through the rough, turbulent sea of the Atlantic is not only a vessel of grief filled with weary bodies and traumatized psyches, but also carries other cargoes: ideas, narratives, feelings, memories, and an assortment of cultural and spiritual content. Furthermore, the slave ship, as the central icon of the Middle Passage, symbolizes the dialectical relationship and transactional entanglement of the three continents in the making of diasporic African identities. The architecture of the ship evokes not just conveyance but confinement, a space of captivity that shattered the illusory hopes for a smooth return from European and American exile. (Fig 09)

By contrast, Aimé Césaire, in his seminal epic poem (a fragment of which is cited above), brings an allegorical force and poetic concreteness to his representation of the Antillean slum, thus bringing forth the social and architectonic disambiguation of slavery. As Césaire's fluorescent lines make clear, the chaos of the Antillean shantytown brought to its knees by poverty and disease— like the sardine-can architecture of the slave ship—is carried from the very beginning of the transatlantic slave trade on the African coast to the shores of American and Caribbean cities and towns. The ship itself allegorizes that principal dialectic of modernity, namely the negotiation of exile and return, enslavement and liberation, captivity and rebellion. It captures the entire human agency of African peoples in the ambivalent sea of modernity. Between sea and land, the oceanic journey spills its guts into spaces filled with ambivalence. How might this ambivalence be scripted? What kind of legibility might it author to describe the lives that Africans made in the Middle Passage, but also the lives that are being made and lived today? This is the challenge of the NMAAHC and the Cape Coast Slavery Museum, which explicitly deal with the legacy of slavery.

14.   The film won the Academy Award for Best Picture in 2014. It was based on the forgotten memoir, *Twelve Years A Slave* (Derby and Miller, 1853), by Solomon Northup (1808–1863), a freeborn African American man from New York who was kidnapped and sold into slavery in the South. Northup's memoir and the dozens of other slave narratives written from the eighteenth through nineteenth centuries have remained the fundamental historical texts that testify to the subjectivity of Africans in Europe and America.

15.   For the use of this term, I am indebted to the influential work of Douglas Crimp on the concepts, histories, and theories of museums, especially the relationship that the concept of the museum establishes between the museal and the mausoleum. In his essay "On the Museum's Ruins," Crimp in turn cites Theodor Adorno, who writes: "The German word *museal* [museumlike] has unpleasant overtones. It describes objects to which the observer no longer has a vital relationship and which are in the process of dying. They owe their preservation more to historical respect than to the needs of the present. Museums and mausoleum are connected by more than phonetic association. Museums are the family sepulchers of works of art." Douglas Crimp, *On the Museum's Ruins* (MIT Press, 1995), p. 44.

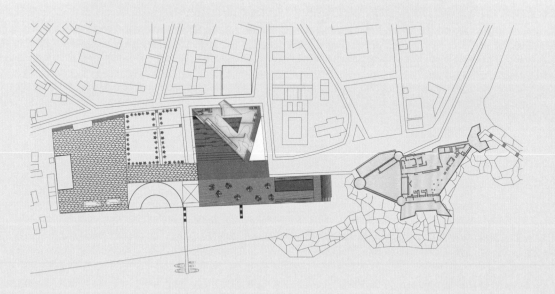

(Fig 06) Cape Coast Castle
Ghana, 18th century
View of the ramparts overlooking the ocean

(Fig 07) CAPE COAST SLAVERY MUSEUM
Cape Coast, Ghana, designed 2012
Site plan showing relationship to Cape Coast Castle

(Fig 08) Thomas Ball (American, 1819–1911)
The Emancipation Monument, 1876
Washington, D.C.

In the next five years, when they are completed between 2016 and 2020, these buildings will face each other across the Atlantic. Not only do the NMAAHC and Cape Coast Slavery Museum mirror each other, they "focus attention on the middle passage," on the quest for "a redemptive return to an African homeland," and on a new symbolic and artifactual script that represents and reimagines African memories in the twenty-first century.[16] It is indeed extremely fortuitous—appropriate, even—that these two buildings, each of which will contain and carry the weight and power of the testimonies of African slaves and their descendants, as well as the burden of the memories left behind, should be designed by Adjaye, an architect born on the African continent and whose family is rooted in Ghana. The two museums respond to more than the quest for redemptive return, they represent a new dialectical bridge between three continents and a dialogical stage from which to explore collective histories of trauma. The NMAAHC and Cape Coast Slavery Museum will stand for two kinds of social vision: the museum as secular shrine and civic sanctuary, and as commemorative totem and mnemonic artifact. In the absence of and failure to construct and constitute memorials and monuments that recognize the sheer scale of suffering and human loss of the slave trade and its legacies, these two buildings, facing each other across the dark, roiling core of the immense ocean—with the water's glassy surface reflecting the fractures, ruptures, and cicatrices of this epic displacement—capture both the distance between Africa and Africans on the opposite shores and the spatial and temporal discontinuities of the trans-Atlantic slave trade. The two museums represent the Atlantic "as one single, complex unit of analysis ... of the modern world."[17]

Here we approach the juncture where the two museums disclose their entangled relation to modernity: with the slave ship as "a living, microcultural, micro-political system in motion" and the African body as commodity deeply embedded in the "economic and historical matrix in which plantation slavery—'capitalism with its clothes off'—was one special moment."[18] Although the two museums are not memorials or monuments per se, they nevertheless respond to the civic absence of the transatlantic slave trade in global symbolic structures. The absence of commemorative structures that recognize the epic history of the transatlantic slave trade and its cultural and social consequences for Africans and the vast communities of its diaspora in Europe, the Americas, and the Caribbean has long haunted both Africa and the West alike. In this sense, the choice of Adjaye as the architect of record in these evolving transactions is especially significant because it brings into high relief the special challenges an African architect faces when called to make buildings of such symbolic power, buildings that respond to the mnemonic violence of slavery without reducing it to a cloying spectacle.

Given this absence, as well as the silence that has concealed the histories and wounds of slavery on world historical memory—especially in a secular culture in which everything is memorialized and musealized—why are these two museums being constructed today, more than a century and a half after the international abolition of slavery and the Emancipation Proclamation in the United States? Surely the construction of the NMAAHC on the National Mall is an ameliorative gesture, emanating from a newfound spirit of civic inclusion. In Cape Coast, on the other hand, to make visible memories and illuminate historical experiences calls

16. Paul Gilroy, *The Black Atlantic: Modernity and Double Consciousness* (Verso, 1993), p. 15.

17. Ibid.

18. Ibid.

attention to African complicity in the slave trade. These narratives have been disremembered and suppressed for too long within Africa itself, where few traces of the fate of the dispossessed are visible. The Cape Coast Slavery Museum and similar spaces, such as the Door of No Return on Goreé Island in Senegal, [Fig 11] offer Africans new opportunities for reconciliation and dialogue with the diaspora.[19]

FROM DIASPORA TO COMMONWEALTH

In pointing to these issues, the principal focus of this essay is therefore not on architecture per se, but on the conditions and spaces of architecture. What are the occasions for the production of architecture? How can the making of architecture and the rhetoric of its production help us understand the relationship between secular culture and civic inclusiveness, and how architecture oscillates between artifact and symbol, structure and sign, along with its various techniques and technologies of immanence within political (democratic) and economic (capitalist) logics? One may ask of any building, but especially of public and civic architecture: what and how does it signify? What kinds of narratives does it construct? What kinds of spaces does it produce? What scripts of identity and identification, subjection and subjectivity does it reproduce and preserve? These questions take on even more urgency when addressed toward the function and signification of public buildings in the context of half a millennium of global migration, colonialism, exile, and diaspora.

Symptoms of this history of global migration include racism, xenophobia, exclusion, and the blocking and limitation of access for minorities and difference. When a new museum, public library, cultural center, or market is constructed in a city with a long history of settling, unsettling, and resettling, what sorts of civic and social constellations can be embedded in its functionality to ameliorate or at least acknowledge the socio-politico-cultural fissures that riddle the urban body politic? What kind of spaces, per Lefebvre, does a public building, or more specifically civic architecture, produce, especially in communities that are in constant flux, or are permanently transitional? Lefebvre offers an important insight here, arguing that "if the gestures of 'spiritual' exchange—the exchange of symbols and signs, with their own peculiar delights, have produced spaces, the gestures of material exchange have been no less productive."[20]

The third building relevant to this discussion is the Stephen Lawrence Centre, constructed to honor the memory of a young Afro-Caribbean Briton who was murdered in a racist attack in 1993. Lawrence's murder galvanized the United Kingdom's African and Caribbean communities to demand greater police response to racially motivated crimes and to insist that municipalities and government agencies address ethnic and racial discrimination and the lack of social amenities and economic opportunities for young black people. Lawrence's murder and the police's initial reluctance to vigorously investigate the perpetrators also exposed the extent to which young black men were deeply vulnerable to juridical ambivalence to their safety and concerns. Rather, the

19.   Over the years many exhibitions, curators, historians, and artists have explored the histories of slavery in powerful and often illuminating ways. A recent exhibition of note on the theme of slavery was based on work by Ndidi Dike, a Nigerian painter and sculptor, and presented in Lagos, Nigeria, at the Centre for Contemporary Art. Entitled *Waka Into Bondage*, this exhibition made an active connection to the history of slavery in Africa, because Lagos was an important slave port from the seventeenth through the eighteenth centuries.

20.   Lefebvre, *The Production of Space*, p. 217.

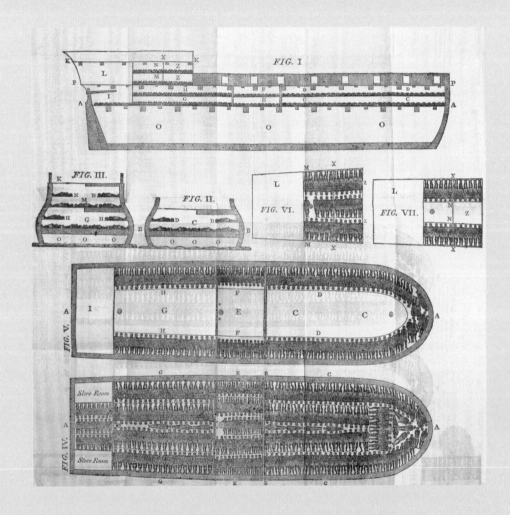

(Fig 09) Society for Effecting the Abolition
of the Slave Trade (British, 1787–1823)
Engraving of the *Brookes*, a British slave ship
showing places for transporting 454 slaves, 1787

entire legal and law enforcement apparatus consistently devoted and deployed its resources toward the criminalization of black men, a response that was exacerbated by the disproportionate and high-handed policing of minority communities.[21] These issues relate to the larger question of how cities are constituted and how architecture imagines the relationship between members of diverse communities. The protests against Lawrence's murder raised and exposed the question of belonging, especially in relation to the uneven recognition of the social well-being of Britain's often marginalized and excluded migrant communities. Adjaye's conception of the Stephen Lawrence Centre took all these issues into account to create a building that serves both as a memorial and a place where life skills and programs on social justice, economic empowerment, and cultural and intellectual agency are the focus. Recognizing the importance of the commemorative function of the center as well as its practical goal to inspire young people across ethnic communities to take charge of their lives and futures, Adjaye Associates describes the project this way:

> The Stephen Lawrence Centre is both a memorial and a place of inspiration in honour of Stephen Lawrence, the architectural student murdered in 1993. … It offers services to the general population of the Lewisham area but has a unique contribution to make in relation to improving the life chances of black Caribbean and African young people. The Centre works closely with partners in the area to tackle underachievement and to increase young people's motivation to embrace education and overcome barriers to fulfillment. The Centre comprises meeting rooms, classrooms, IT labs, offices, and exhibition spaces.[22]

What needs to be underlined is the vital connection between these three buildings and the inclusion of African memories in the social landscape of global architectural concepts. The issue that must be faced in the massive expansion of global architecture is not simply the functionalist and theoretical modeling of discourses of architecture, but the political, social, and cultural visions of buildings. How can public and civic architecture go beyond engaging its users with amenities and instead fundamentally realign and reorient the devices of power toward users' aspirations, toward creating a community, framing the conditions of shared citizenship, of *res publica*—the commonwealth of diverse social and cultural experiences? The postcolonial, cosmopolitan, and multicultural tilt of many cities exposes the inadequacy of much current public and civic architectural discourse to create spaces that explore and serve this rising global commonwealth. This inadequacy frequently becomes even more visible in museums, which too often appeal to the desires and aspirations of their patrons rather than identify with the multicultural and transnational public sphere. But it may well be that it is in the process of producing public and civic architecture that the opportunity to examine the rift between migrants and indigenes emerges. These instances can offer moments to analyze the paradoxes of commemoration, foster the processes of re-membering, and bind old wounds to the tissue of historical experience and living memory. Gilroy's image of the slave ship offers a model of thinking diasporically in the present. It is due to multiple historical convergences that, as Adjaye attained the intellectual stature he had worked hard to achieve, he was entrusted with the design of some of the most significant

21.   See "Report of the Stephen Lawrence Inquiry," Sir William MacPherson, Feb. 1999, http://www.archive.official-documents.co.uk/document/cm42/4262/sli-00.htm.

22.   See "Stephen Lawrence Centre," http://www.adjaye.com/projects/civic-buildings/stephen-lawrence-centre/.

(Fig 10) CAPE COAST SLAVERY MUSEUM
Cape Coast, Ghana, designed 2012
View from the shore showing the exterior space
protected by the museum, rendering

(Fig 11) The Door of No Return
Gorée Island, Senegal, c. 1776

and symbolically freighted buildings that deeply bind Africa and its vast but scattered diaspora in Europe and the Americas. At every opportunity, Adjaye has made the gestures of affiliation connecting these spaces powerfully resonant in buildings that are new and contemporary. The lessons of his architecture therefore do not lie merely in the formal ideas that constitute his architectural language, but also in their social and political significance. His distinctive use of form to create symbolic and representational experiences that connect the real and the imaginary is powerfully balanced by his subtle political imagination. Given his persistent quest to balance the artistic and the political, the aesthetic and the ethical, abstraction and representation, Adjaye has come to the conclusion that we can and should ask more of architecture.

URI
SYST

AN
EMS

SUGAR HILL
New York, 2011–14
Aerial view with Sugar Hill on left

David Adjaye has been practicing as an architect for over twenty years, and throughout this period his design work has borne some relationship to the city. When he began to teach architecture soon after graduating, the distinctive development patterns in various parts of London were a constant reference. He opened his first office in the heart of the East End, where he thought it might be easier to construct new buildings than in affluent west London, where he had worked as an assistant when he was a student. His first projects, small restaurants and bars within existing buildings, were conceived as external spaces of a kind that might be found in a more tidy city than London then was—perhaps a city in continental Europe. As he had hoped, his first major public building was a civic hub, the Idea Store Whitechapel, whose top-floor café enjoys panoramic views of London's skyline. Developing out of this work, the Museum of Contemporary Art Denver was conceived as a fragment of pedestrian city within a building, and for the Moscow School of Management Skolkovo, located in an outer suburb of the Russian capital, he designed a building with the attributes of a small city. Since then he has been responsible for multiple projects in Washington, D.C., New Orleans, and New York in which his appreciation of the history and social life of these places has played an essential role in the buildings' composition and detailing.

Adjaye's approach in the explicitly urban projects is related to their scale. Sugar Hill, Hallmark Towers, and One Berkeley Street are fragments of renewal in well-established environments; they include a range of urban functions, and their architecture develops connections with the surrounding areas. In a second group, the primary spatial objective is to create a contemporary urban space. Examples include Piety Bridge and Piety Wharf in New Orleans, which give views of the city that were previously difficult to obtain, and the Art Campus Tel Aviv, where a new square is tied into the surrounding area by a series of smaller spaces. At neighborhood level, Al Kahraba Street, Elmina College, and Hackney Fashion Hub involved the construction of spatial infrastructures that include sites that can be developed with some independence. In each case, the organization of the infrastructure and the nature of the infill respond to the local context. At the largest scale, the master-plan projects involve the development and coordination of several spatial infrastructures to address the wider needs of a community. Adjaye designs key buildings in these proposals to indicate the overall objectives he has in mind.

In architectural terms, the urban projects fall into three main types. Where there is a public element to the program, the external profile of the building and the positioning of the public entrance reflect this, while other aspects of the design connect with the context. In the projects based on repetition and dealing with retail or residential units, the architecture is primarily concerned with continuing and developing the urban landscape. Lastly, Elmina College and the master-plan proposals involve the creation of new urban landscapes that have the capacity to include a wide range of facilities, each with its own expression. They make strategic connections with context and suggest new identities for the cities in which they are located.

SUGAR HILL
New York, 2011–14
Front facade with entrance to Children's Museum of Art
and Storytelling (right) and to early childhood center
and apartments (left)

SUGAR HILL
New York, 2011-14
The long gallery in the Children's Museum of Art
and Storytelling

Interior view of early childhood center

Interior view of apartment

Section

MOSCOW SCHOOL OF MANAGEMENT SKOLKOVO
Moscow, 2006–10
Aerial view in winter

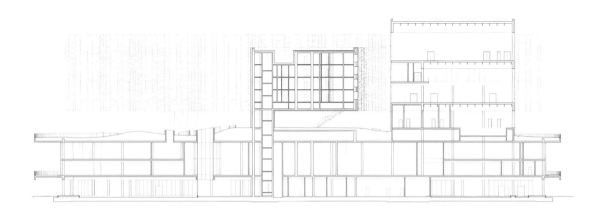

MOSCOW SCHOOL OF MANAGEMENT SKOLKOVO
Moscow, 2006-10
Radial view inside "disc" element

Section

Main auditorium

PIETY BRIDGE & PIETY WHARF
New Orleans, 2008-14
View of Piety Bridge looking toward the
Mississippi River and the gable wall
of Piety Wharf

ALARA CONCEPT STORE
Lagos, Nigeria, 2011—14
Front facade

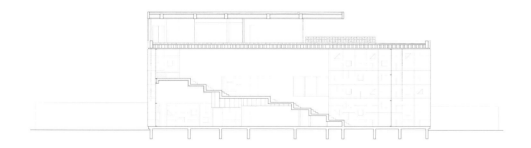

Interior view from the top floor

Section

AÏSHTI FOUNDATION
Beirut, Lebanon, 2012–15
View from the coastal highway, rendering

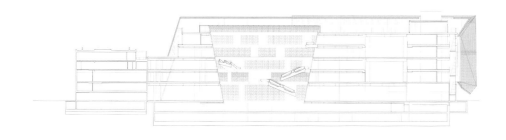

Section showing retail space (left)
and art space (right)

AL KAHRABA STREET
Doha, Qatar, designed 2010
Rendering of office building with Al Kahraba Street on right

Construction view

Site plan showing block structure

ELMINA COLLEGE
Elmina, Ghana, designed 2009
Main entrance to the teaching center, rendering

View of teaching center showing arcades and
refectory (on right), rendering

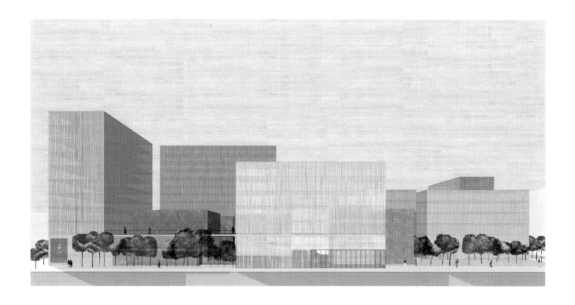

CULTURAL CAMPUS FRANKFURT
Frankfurt, Germany, designed 2010
Exterior view showing the city within a city, rendering

Interior view, rendering

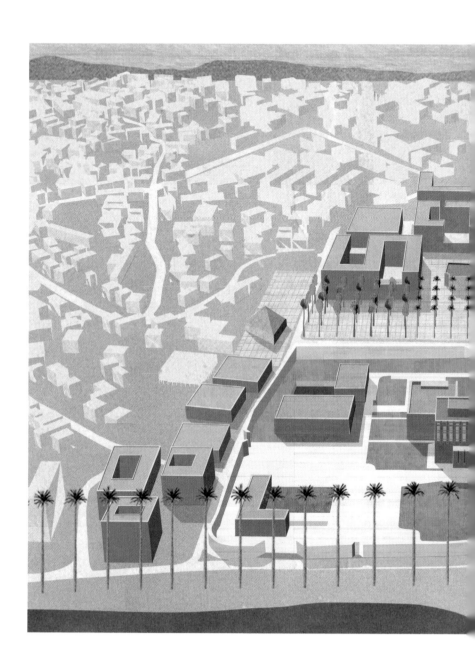

GOVERNMENT QUARTER MASTER PLAN
Libreville, Gabon, designed 2012
Aerial view from ocean, rendering

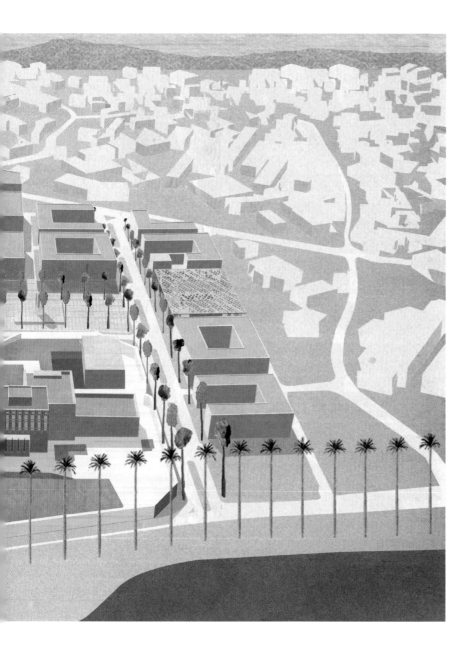

ONE BERKELEY STREET
London, designed 2013
Street view showing position of
main entrance, rendering

ART CAMPUS TEL AVIV
Tel Aviv, Israel, designed 2013
View showing new urban square, rendering

HACKNEY FASHION HUB
London, designed 2013
Plan showing retail space under railway viaduct

Reoccupied railway viaduct, rendering

Development of corner sites, rendering

HALLMARK TOWERS
Johannesburg, South Africa, designed 2013
Front facade, rendering

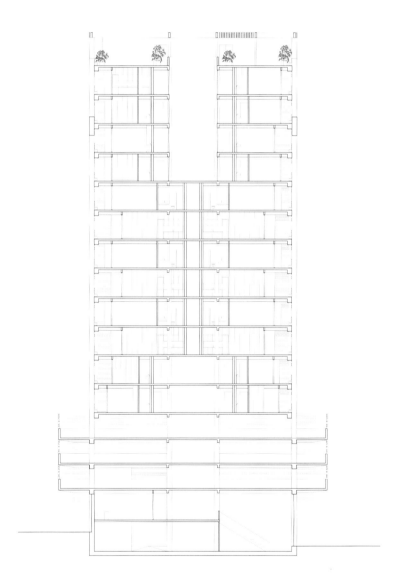

Section

NAKAWA MASTER PLAN
Nakawa, Kampala, Uganda, designed 2013
Site plan

View of central park showing cluster
of ten office towers, rendering

View of central park from
ten-tower cluster, rendering

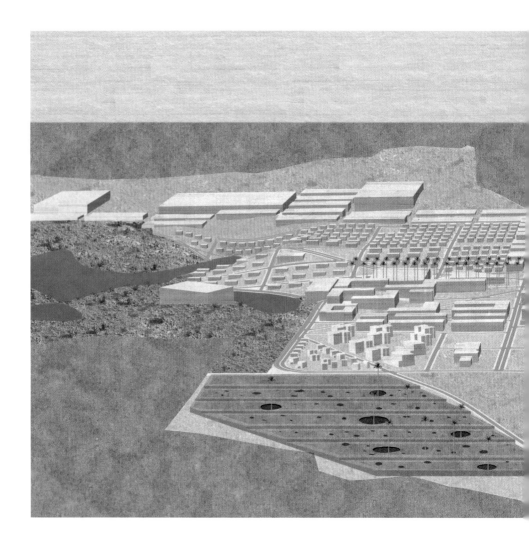

PETRONIA MASTER PLAN
Petronia, Ghana, designed 2013

Aerial view showing central business district
on right, rendering

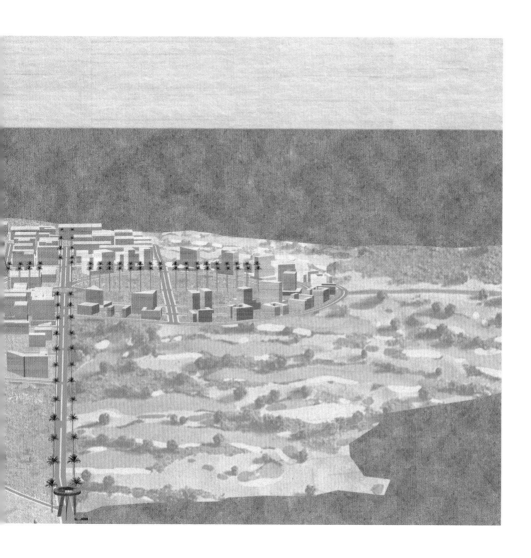

Observation deck at junction
of approach roads, rendering

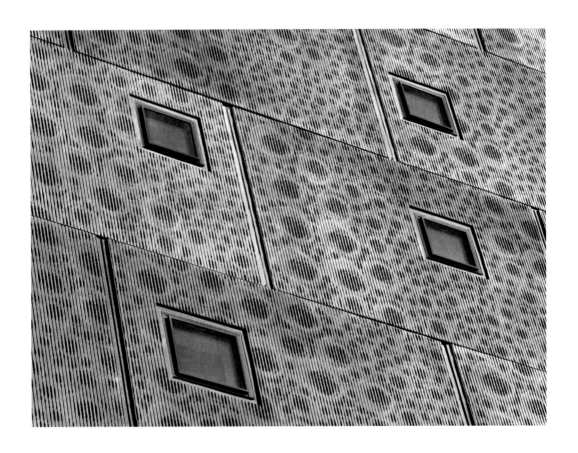

SUGAR HILL
New York, 2011-14
Detail of facade

READING
THE CITY

PETER ALLISON

(Fig 01) *David Adjaye: Making Public Buildings*
Exhibition at Whitechapel Gallery, London, 2006
View with models of Bernie Grant Arts Centre
auditorium building in foreground

(Fig 02) LUNCH @ EXMOUTH MARKET
London, 1997
Adjaye and Russell Architects (active 1994-2000)
The interior as a continuation of the exterior

(Fig 03) *Urban Investigations*
An exhibition of Unit 4 work at the
Architecture Foundation, London, 2006

A distinctive feature of David Adjaye's working method is his reuse of spatial concepts and forms of construction in different projects. For example, two of his pavilions, <u>Asymmetric Chamber</u> (which appeared in Manchester and New York) and <u>Length × Width × Height</u> (which appeared in London), are concerned with the experience of linear spaces and how such spaces are constructed. London's <u>Lost House</u> and <u>Idea Store Chrisp Street</u>, and the <u>Alara Concept Store</u> in Lagos, Nigeria, all developed out of these experiments. The later pavilions employ a form of timber construction that results in continuously slotted walls. Similar solid/void patterns can be seen in the facades of <u>Rivington Place</u> in London, the <u>Francis A. Gregory Library</u> in Washington, D.C., and the <u>Aïshti Foundation</u> in Beirut, Lebanon. This way of working can be said to have a typological basis, in that it involves a repertoire of identifiable components, conceived with some general purpose in mind but progressively adapted to address new conditions. The following notes concern Adjaye's design responses to urban situations and their typological basis.

"CITYSPACE"

A concern with the city has informed Adjaye's architecture since he set up his first office. As a recently qualified architect, he supplemented his income by lecturing part time at London Southbank University, where he ran an undergraduate design studio with Mike Kane. The studio was known as Unit 4 and, for the three years of its existence, the teaching program focused on the relationship between urbanism and architecture.[01] (Fig 03) Two of the projects for the 1994–95 academic year were titled *Exchange* and *Theatre*. For *Exchange*, the students surveyed the blocks in the vicinity of Portobello Road in west London, paying attention to the way in which the exchange of "information, goods, emotions, beliefs, (and) celebrations" had colonized the small infill sites left by the Victorian terraced housing.[02] Each student then attempted to emulate this process—tailoring usage to the urban fabric, rather than vice versa—on a site of her or his choosing. *Theatre* did not involve the design of an actual theater but was based on looking at "the city as a theatre of activities played out in the public realm."[03] In the first phase the students analyzed the sense of place in one of a series of 50 × 500 meter strips covering the length of the southern bank of the Thames between Waterloo and Blackfriars Bridges. Based on this analysis, each student selected a site and designed a public building with the specific intention that its architecture should reflect the sense of place at that location.[04]

01.   The author thanks Mike Kane of KMK Architects, London, for the opportunity to discuss Unit 4.

02.   David Adjaye and Mike Kane, *Unit 4 1994/95, Student Work* (Self-published, 1995), p. 3, KMK Archive.

03.   Ibid., p. 1.

04.   The students' projects were shown in *Urban Investigations*, an exhibition at the Architecture Foundation, London, July 14–23, 1995.

Adjaye and Kane continued to develop their city-based program the following academic year and, in an introduction to the work of the studio written in September 1996, they summarized their position in a text titled "Cityspace."[05] For them, the city is liberating: "Cityspace does not assume particular behaviors in us, it defies conventions and encourages a connected diversity. It reveals the possibility of experiences outside ourselves." Such experiences are often connected with social change, which may create new opportunities for designers. As they explained, "The Western city has stopped expanding and is in a period of internal diversity and change. Contemporary readings of the life of cities acknowledge this as a place of flux, a catalyst for change based on perceptions from the street. The street is the place of the chance encounter; lacking an easy definition, it allows the freedom from conventions of form and function." The second half of "Cityspace" concerns the studio's response to the urban conditions they identified. "The Unit explores an architecture of spatial connectiveness located in cityspaces with the potential for invigoration. The fabrication of space, based on non-utilitarian methods of definition, allows the design process to free itself from the limiting conventions of function and the comforts of familiarity."

In the project in the Portobello Road area, the students' sites were small enclosures hemmed in by larger buildings and boundary walls. Under the influence of their teachers, their design proposals made a point of revealing the full extent of their sites and employed materials that contrasted with the existing structures. A similar approach to site and materiality can be seen in the cafés and bars that Adjaye designed in central London in the 1990s: existing buildings were hollowed out and then reoccupied as if they were small courtyards.[Fig 02] A key design move in most of these projects was the removal of the lower section of the front or back wall of the existing building so that it could be replaced by a glazed opening. Later examples, such as Elektra House and Seven, in London and New York, respectively, incorporate similar moves in new structures.

MAKING PUBLIC BUILDINGS

Having designed a clutch of buildings located within walking distance of London's Whitechapel Gallery, Adjaye was invited to show his work there, and the resulting exhibition, *Making Public Buildings*, opened in early 2006.[06][Fig 01] It focused on ten of his public buildings and gave prominence to certain aspects of the design process. In the main space the buildings were shown on separate benches, where each of them was represented by three models: a 1:500 scale model showing the existing buildings in the vicinity of the site; a 1:100 model showing the internal configuration of the new building, and a 1:50 model showing the exterior of the new building in some detail. In the catalogue, one page per project was devoted to the site concept, which was demonstrated in a series of isometric drawings showing, step by step, how the form of the project had been modified in direct response to neighboring streets and buildings.[Fig 04] Each of these drawings was accompanied by explanatory notes and a corresponding view of the detailed model or completed building. The internal spatial configuration was shown in a drawing of the assembly of volumes.[Fig 05]

05.   David Adjaye and Mike Kane, "Cityspace," handout for Unit 4 1996/97, Sept. 1996, p. 2, KMK Archive. The following quotations are also from this text.

06.   The exhibition *David Adjaye, Making Public Buildings*, was on view at Whitechapel Gallery, London, January 24–March 26, 2006. See David Adjaye, Peter Allison, Okwui Enwezor, et al., *Making Public Buildings: Specificity, Customization, Imbrication*, exh. cat. (Whitechapel Gallery/Thames and Hudson, 2006).

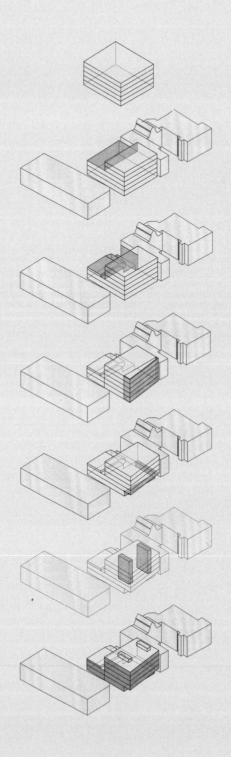

(Fig 04) IDEA STORE WHITECHAPEL
London, 2001–05
Site-concept drawings as published in the
exhibition catalogue for *Making Public Buildings*

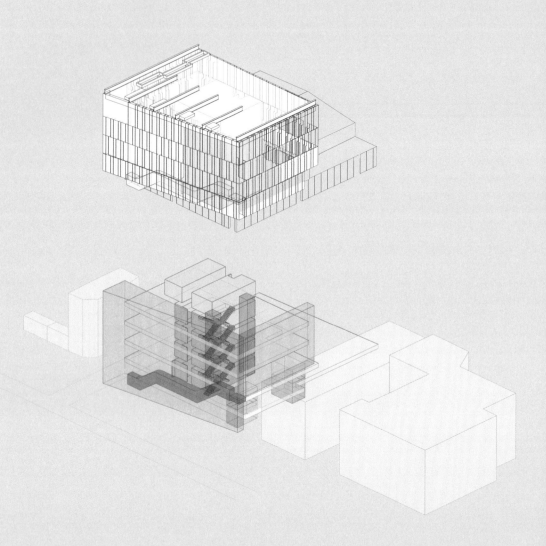

(Fig 05) IDEA STORE WHITECHAPEL
London, 2001–05
Facade-system drawing and assembly-of-volumes drawing
as published in the exhibition catalogue
for *Making Public Buildings*

In general, these public buildings display similar characteristics to those anticipated in *Theatre*. In London's Idea Store Whitechapel, for instance, the pattern of movement and display found in the adjacent street market informed the internal planning, giving the impression that the organization of the building is a response to the context, rather than merely the practical requirements of the brief. The implication behind the analysis of the 50 × 500 meter strips in *Theatre* was that sense of place is not static but in a process of constant evolution at the micro level. If a new building is to conform to this analysis, its external appearance requires a materiality that makes a clear distinction between new and old, as in Adjaye's interior courtyard projects of the 1990s. On the other hand, it is desirable to develop continuity with the surroundings so as not to disrupt the sense of place. The exteriors of the buildings in the exhibition demonstrated a variety of ways in which this dichotomy can be resolved. Light-absorbing finishes, muted reflections, shifting grids, and pierced screens were employed to ensure that innovative forms rejoin the continuum of the city. Internally, these buildings set up multiple views of their surroundings, enhancing users' awareness of the urban location.

As shown in the site-concept drawings, Adjaye intends that his buildings enjoy a reciprocal relationship with their neighbors so that, in an echo of the idea put forward by British architects Alison and Peter Smithson in the 1950s, they function together as a unified "cluster."[07](Fig 06) The Smithsons explain their use of the term as follows: "The word 'cluster' meaning a specific pattern of association has been introduced to replace such group concepts as street, town, city (group entities), which are too loaded with historical overtones. Any coming together is cluster. Cluster is a sort of clearing-house term during the period of creation of new types." It is possible to identify at least four types of cluster in the exhibition material, and developments of these types can be seen in Adjaye's later projects, such as One Berkeley Street. (Fig 07) Buildings can engage with the cluster concept by addressing existing urban frontages, by working with their neighbors to define urban spaces, by forming a cluster themselves, by integrating with a landscape, or by adopting several of these options at once.

URBAN FRONTAGES

According to the Smithsons, the problem of building "in an existing street is one of finding a way (while still responding to the street idea) to chop through the old building face and build up a complex in depth, of providing a suggestion, a sign, of the new community structure."[08] Employing different means than those available to the Smithsons, the Whitechapel and Chrisp Street Idea Stores and Rivington Place, all in the East End of London, respond to these requirements. Their facades continue the scale and rhythm of the adjoining frontages; the entrance spaces cut through the section of the building, revealing the depth of the site and the organization of the interior, and by taking clues from the larger clusters in which they are situated, these buildings possess a presence that suggests a "new community structure."

Adjaye's recent frontage projects are more widely dispersed. In Washington, D.C., the Francis A. Gregory Library is part of a cluster of community facilities that do not stand in close proximity but are connected with one another by Alabama Avenue, which passes in front of the building. With a school to the west and a shopping center to the east, the open tube defined by

07.   Alison and Peter Smithson quoted in Theo Crosby and Nigel Henderson, *Uppercase* 3 (Whitefriars, 1961), quoted in Alison and Peter Smithson, *The Charged Void: Urbanism* (Monacelli, 2005), p. 30. Peter Smithson taught Adjaye when he was a postgraduate student at the Royal College of Art in London.

08.   Alison and Peter Smithson, "Cluster City," *Architectural Review* (Nov. 1957), p. 336.

the front of the building and the overhanging roof makes an architectural connection between its otherwise separate neighbors. Similarly, the Aïshti Foundation is located on a brownfield site between a ten-lane coastal highway and the shore of the Mediterranean Sea. By forming a barrier against the road, the building protects a new public space on the waterfront. As well as shading the building's walls and roof, the strong pattern of the external latticework identifies the structure to passing traffic and softens the appearance of the sea-facing facade, which would otherwise reflect an unwelcome amount of sunlight.

URBAN SPACES

Defining shared open space is the most obvious consequence of placing buildings in a cluster, but there are many ways of doing this. The Bernie Grant Arts Centre in Tottenham in north London, was an addition to an existing cluster that needed to encourage public access to an area that had previously been sealed off by the older buildings. This was achieved by forming a new public square, situated within a network of landscaped connections. The relationship between the square and the design of the auditorium building's foyer ensure that the Bernie Grant Arts Centre has an equivalent standing to the other institutions that constitute this extended campus. By contrast, in the Wakefield Market Hall in Wakefield in the United Kingdom, the fully enclosed elements in the brief are grouped around a space for the open market, which forms a portico to the adjacent bus terminal. As well as protecting the market, the oversailing roof continues the line of the street in the absence of a facade.

Two types of clusters play a role in the Al Kahraba Street project for Doha, Qatar. Sometimes referred to as "A Street in Doha," Adjaye's proposal involves eight blocks on either side of the street, whose continuity is maintained by the frontages of his buildings. But the area he is responsible for is a relatively small part of a more extensive development, and the block structure is intended to be highly permeable to allow movement in all directions. With this in mind, the project was conceived as a single built volume from which a variety of external spaces are excavated: passageways, formal and informal courtyards, recessed areas at ground level for shade, private terraces for apartments, and the gently curving street.[09]

The Art Campus Tel Aviv in Tel Aviv, Israel also employs a cluster strategy to define a series of open spaces in order to establish strong links between the new development and the surrounding area. The main elements of the program are arranged in a U-shape to create an enclosed plaza on an east-west axis with Yesod HaMa'ala Street. The theater, dance studios, and community building are kept slightly separate so each retains its identity, and the gaps between them give access to the plaza, where food and drink will be served. A tree-planted courtyard to the north makes a spatial connection with Minshar for Art—a separate institution—and the open area to the east can be used as a market square. In Adjaye's Cultural Campus Frankfurt proposal for Frankfurt, Germany, a similar range of external spaces are laid out on a more abstract basis, as the location of the site is still under discussion.

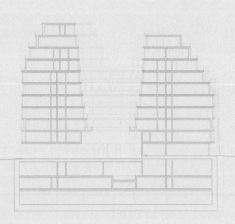

(Fig 06) Alison and Peter Smithson
(British, 1928-1993 and 1923-2003)
The Economist Building, London, 1964
Three-building cluster

(Fig 07) ONE BERKELEY STREET
London, designed 2013
Section

Working with similar concerns, but no actual buildings, Piety Wharf is a riverside enclosure where the people of New Orleans can enjoy a direct experience of the Mississippi. With the scale and surfaces of a small public square, it contrasts with the linear park that has replaced a line of old wharves. Isolated from nearby streets by a railway, Piety Bridge is one of two access points to the new park, its bold form signaling the presence of the open space. Piety Wharf is the area enclosed by Corten steel walls, screens, and parapets, which stands on the timber structure that supported the original wharf. Its perimeter wall hides the open view of the center of the city, which is then revealed in stages as visitors move into the main space and through an opening in an old gable wall. The scale of the enclosure recalls the volume of the storage shed that once stood here, and its configuration celebrates the drama of New Orleans's relationship to the river.

FORMING BUILDINGS

In a limited number of Adjaye's projects, the cluster configuration occurs within, or partially within, the building itself. In the Museum of Contemporary Art Denver (MCAD), the gallery spaces are located in three independent volumes that define a T-shaped atrium. These volumes are in turn enclosed by a peripheral ambulatory. This whole arrangement was intended to establish a pedestrian-friendly environment, suitable for experiencing art, of a kind that is otherwise more likely found in medieval cities. Although they have seldom been published together, the external volume of the neighboring LN House is a similar height to the three volumes containing the MCAD's galleries. Standing alongside the museum, the house can be seen as a fourth component of the cluster.

A similar attempt to bring additional intensity to an unexpected location can be seen in the William O. Lockridge Library in Washington, D.C. On a gentle rise, the site has much to recommend it, but it is a block away from the main thoroughfare, where many services are housed. By allocating key spaces to three separate volumes and clustering them around an open space that forms an entrance to the building, the library appears to be a collection of buildings, distinguishing it from the nearby houses and suggesting that it is a local center. The three volumes also have a decisive effect on the interior, offering separate spaces for children, teens, and adults in an intermediate zone between the body of the library and the surrounding streets.

LANDSCAPE

The majority of projects featured in *Making Public Buildings* are in relatively dense urban settings, the two exceptions being the TBA21 Pavilion, which at that time was on a small island in the Venetian Lagoon, and London's Stephen Lawrence Centre, which is located in a park running alongside a tributary of the Thames. The latter building comprises two triangular-shaped volumes whose faces address a variety of conditions in the surrounding landscape—mature trees, the river, a formal garden, and an entrance court. The exterior's oblique corners and metal-mesh cladding reduce the building's visual solidity, integrating it within the landscape.

In comparable situations, Adjaye has employed circular volumes to similar effect. The Moscow School of Management Skolkovo is situated in the valley of the Setun River on the outskirts of the Russian capital, and the building was concentrated at the center of the site to minimize the area given over to construction. The circular form of the structure's disc element maintains a degree of continuity on the site and allows the interior to enjoy views in every direction. Similarly, the desire to create a 360-degree view explains the circular form of the MEMO—Mass Extinction Monitoring Observatory project, standing in the historically significant landscape of England's Jurassic Coast. The Portland stone construction extends the materiality of the landscape into the building itself, asserting a connection between the building, the cliffs on which it stands, and the view. A coastal perspective is also the inspiration for the Cape Coast Slavery Museum in Cape Coast, Ghana. It overlooks an eighteenth-century slave fort—the source of its solid, triangular form—but a sense of lightness was achieved by cantilevering the main volume above a raked gathering area.

Certain aspects of the National Museum of African American History and Culture (NMAAHC) can also be explained by reference to the landscape cluster type. The museum is located on the dividing line between the formality of the architectural composition to the east (the Mall, with the other Smithsonian museums on either side, terminating in the US Capitol) and the commemorative landscape to the west, where protests and rallies take place (the axis of the Mall continued by the Reflecting Pool and a planted area extending to the Potomac River). This duality is reflected in the interplay between the building's square-shaped volume and the faceted cladding of its Corona. The plan position of the facades continues the alignment of the adjacent museum buildings and terminates this sequence in response to the cross-axis on which the White House is located. Moreover, the perforated bronze-coated cladding of the Corona possesses the light-responsive characteristics of the metal mesh on the Stephen Lawrence Centre, and the angle at which it tilts forward is taken from the Washington Monument, the most prominent structure in the memorial park. By responding directly to both the architectural context and the adjacent landscape, Adjaye's design acknowledges the unique position of the NMAAHC within the larger composition of which it is an integral part.

AFRICAN METROPOLITAN ARCHITECTURE & EUROPOLIS

Adjaye's first study visit to an African city was to Lusaka, Zambia, in 2000. By 2006 he had photographed several more cities and, invited to curate an exhibition at the Graduate School of Design at Harvard University in Cambridge, Massachusetts, proposed using this material as the subject. The exhibition took place in 2007 and included ten cities, which were grouped on the wall according to their position on the continent.[10] (Fig 09) To facilitate comparisons, the images of each city were presented under three headings: civic, commercial, and residential. The majority of the photographs related to the "formal" city, in which buildings employ conventional forms of construction, but there was a significant number relating to the "informal" city, in which makeshift construction predominates. A horizontal division ran through the presentation of all ten cities, with the images of the formal city arranged by category above the line, and images of the informal city placed below it. The introductory material for each city included an aerial view, a layout drawing of the central area, and a selection of statistical information.

The exhibition was well received and resulted in an invitation to prepare a book on the same subject, which was published in 2011 under the title African Metropolitan Architecture.[11]

10.   The exhibition was titled *African Cities: A Photographic Survey by David Adjaye*, and was held at Gund Hall Gallery, Harvard University, Cambridge, Massachusetts, April 2–May 23, 2007. The ten cities were Accra, Ghana; Addis Ababa, Ethiopia; Nairobi, Kenya; Pretoria, South Africa; Harare, Zimbabwe; Asmara, Eritrea; Bamako, Mali; Ouagadougou, Burkina Faso; Abidjan, Côte d'Ivoire; and Dakar, Senegal.

11.   David Adjaye, *African Metropolitan Architecture*, ed. Peter Allison (Rizzoli, 2011), also published as *Adjaye, Africa, Architecture: A Photographic Survey of Metropolitan Architecture* (Thames and Hudson, 2011).

(Fig 08) AFRICAN METROPOLITAN ARCHITECTURE, 2000–11
Spread from the Forest volume showing civic
buildings in Kampala, Uganda, pp. 100–01

(Fig 09) *African Cities: A Photographic Survey by David Adjaye*
Exhibition at the Graduate School of Design,
Harvard University, Cambridge, Massachusetts, 2007

CIVIC / The city's civic architecture is dominated by the grand mosque, cathedral and sikh temple, all with prominent steeples and towers. This signifies the multicultural nature of Kampala. The public buildings are late-modernist institutions with austere facades, protected by shading systems and screens.

KAMPALA / UGANDA FOREST

100/101

Taking a lead from the exhibition, the book organized the continent's capital cities according to their position in one of six geographic terrains: the Maghreb, Desert, the Sahel, Savanna and Grassland, Forest, and Mountain and Highveld. Cities in the same terrain share similar conditions such as height above sea level, climate, and vegetation, while the topography, history, and relative economic standing are specific to each place. Assembled on the page under the three headings employed in the exhibition—civic, commercial, and residential—Adjaye's images record the on-the-ground consequences of these basic conditions. (Fig 08) They also provide information on the size and density of the cities, the relationship between center and suburbs, the pattern of everyday life, and the expression of different cultures. Placed alongside aerial views and drawings of the spatial infrastructure in central areas, this material offers a structured overview of the urban situation in the continent.

The Europolis study applies a similarly structured view to another continent. Invited to participate in Manifesta 7, an art biennial in Bolzano, Italy, held in 2008, Adjaye prepared a composite drawing in which Europe's capital cities were moved closer together, forming a single conurbation that would be larger than any existing city but far smaller than Europe. (Fig 10) In Bolzano the drawing was presented as an ocher-colored metallic foil laminate, sandwiched between two sheets of glass to form a freestanding panel that could be viewed from both sides. For his own purposes, Adjaye also completed a set of thematic drawings showing the various components of Europolis—main roads, waterways, green spaces, flight paths, public transit, development textures—as separate elements. (Fig 11) The surprising outcome of both the Africa and Europolis studies was that the act of presenting the cities in a structure that places them in close proximity clarifies their differences. Combining photographs representing African cities or drawing a composite of the infrastructure pattern of European cities suggested the unique experiences that each city has to offer, rather than emphasizing their similarities.

URBAN SYSTEMS

With the advent of high-speed travel, it could be argued that European cities can be sampled in the manner suggested by the Europolis drawing, and that the drawing only confirms a shift in perception that has already occurred. Placing the cities in close proximity does, however, suggest possibilities over and above those currently available, and combining conditions that were previously separate can be seen as a design move with considerable potential. This strategy is employed in the design of the Moscow School of Management Skolkovo, in response to questions raised by the original brief. The school was always intended to form part of a larger development, including a science university and a technology park, and it therefore needed to be located where there was sufficient land. In practice, this led to a site located just outside the last of the city's major ring roads. To counter the drawback of an innovatory institution being situated at such a remove from the central area, Adjaye developed the building as a small city, in which facilities that would normally be laid out horizontally form a vertical stack. Movement and services are at ground level, social and business activities are located in the disc element, and living and recreation occupy the superstructure. It is a city of which El Lissitzky himself might have approved: its presence registers in Moscow, in Russia, and internationally—as the founders required—and its form is open to future development.[12]

12.   The Russian Suprematist artist El Lissitzky proposed *Proun*, a concept of reality that he illustrated in a series of paintings and drawings made between 1919 and 1923. Some of them include radiating rectangular solids floating above a circle.

(Fig 10) EUROPOLIS, 2008
The composite drawing presented as
a freestanding panel at the Manifesta 7
biennial, Bolzano, Italy, 2008

(Fig 11) EUROPOLIS, 2008
Drawing showing development textures

The conditions under which the Skolkovo project was developed and realized have so far been exceptional in Adjaye's oeuvre, but the programmatic layering of contrasting functional zones has been a feature of several recent proposals. Sugar Hill in New York's Harlem is sometimes described as a residential project, but the early childhod center and children's museum, which occupy two levels of the podium, are significant additions to the social fabric in their own right. The scale of the podium relates to the adjoining streets and buildings, while the slab above takes its place in Manhattan's skyline.

The One Berkeley Street building also combines spatial paradigms from separate sources. In response to its location on a historic thoroughfare in central London, the aboveground section is divided into two parts. The organization of the lower floors, including shops and a hotel, is similar to the nineteenth-century shopping arcades found in this part of London. With a different orientation, the upper floors, which are given over to apartments, follow the example of the eighteenth-century residential courtyards in the area. On the street facades, which are subject to strict control, the difference between the upper and lower levels is played down, within a strategy that retains the capacity to make certain distinctions. While the edge of the structural frame follows the site boundary, the scalloped walls are concave (toward the street) and stone clad on the lower floors, and convex and bronze clad above. The length of the horizontal bays varies in response to the visual characteristics of the surrounding streets, and the rhythms of successive floors unite the upper and lower sections of the facades.

MASTER PLANS

Adjaye's first foray into master planning concerned a temporary building for Frieze Art Fair. In London, Frieze is housed in an aluminium-framed, air-conditioned tent in Regents Park, and Adjaye was responsible for the internal layout of the fair for the first three years of its existence, starting in 2003. His design exhibits many of the attributes of an ancient Greek city: a grid of thoroughfares giving access to larger and smaller areas for the dealers, small squares for public gatherings, a performance space, and places for refreshment. (Fig 12) The detailed arrangements within these spaces were not Adjaye's concern, as the purpose of his scheme was to provide an organizational framework in which a variety of possibilities could be freely accommodated. A more architectural version of this type of organization can be seen in the proposal for Elmina College in Elmina, Ghana. In African Metropolitan Architecture, Adjaye discusses the role of roof architecture in the Forest terrain, where this project is located. Roofs have deep overhangs for protection from tropical storms and for shade when the sun is shining. The spatial infrastructure of Elmina College is defined by a continuous roof, set in a tropical landscape and punctuated by planted courtyards. As in the Frieze Art Fair project, this arrangement allows for considerable freedom in the disposition of individual spaces.

Similar concerns inform the master plans for sites in Libreville in Gabon, Kampala in Uganda, and for the new "energy city" of Petronia, near Takoradi, about 140 miles west of Accra in Ghana.[13] In all cases, Adjaye employed a planning grid as a basis for proposing a pattern of development that includes an appropriate range of conditions to meet the needs of the future community. On a sloping twenty-seven-hectare site in the Nakawa area of Kampala, the grid provides a framework within which the residential density can be increased or decreased,

13.   Petronia is intended to be the first city in West Africa able to meet its own energy needs, as well as supply the national grid.

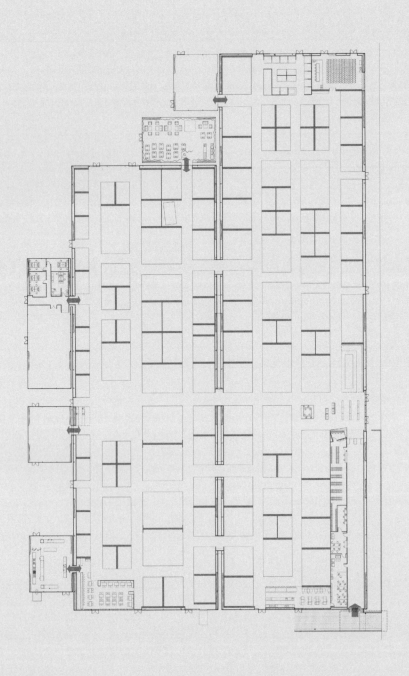

(Fig 12) FRIEZE ART FAIR
London, 2003
Layout plan showing circulation
routes and gallery spaces

depending on the character of the surrounding neighborhoods, the capacity of the local infrastructure, and landscape considerations. The grid breaks and changes direction in response to adjacent roads, and the center of the site is left open as "a green lung."[14] The center of Kampala lies to the west, and this end of the site is the setting for an iconic tower—ten inverted cones in a circular cluster. A parking facility and transport interchange is housed in an undercroft below the tower: an arrangement that supports retail and commercial uses in the nearby streets.

In each of the master plan projects, the dimensions of the grid have been employed to calculate the sizes of different types of building, the number of people they might accommodate, the infrastructure capacity required, and so on. Apart from addressing logistical considerations, the grids are intended to clarify the conditions under which the development process and architecture can flourish. The range of grids employed in Petronia—corresponding to a central business district, a mixed-use commercial zone, a civic and cultural zone, and residential areas—are based on an understanding of the contribution that contrasting grids have made to the development of African cities. They interact with the topography of the site, with landscapes and routes, and set up relationships with them, both in general and in detail. All of the urban strategies that Adjaye has utilized in earlier projects will be relevant somewhere in the grid.

The brief for the Government Quarter Master Plan in Libreville, Gabon, envisages a new government center in an area where the existing streets have no clear order. This situation was addressed in the first phase proposal, which rationalizes the positions of key buildings. The effective seat of government is the old presidential palace, whose front facade faces inland, preventing a direct connection between the new center and the ocean. Adjaye has resolved this dilemma with the placement of the new public space: it connects the central axis, between the old palace and the new government buildings, with twin axes located on either side of the palace, which continue to the waterfront. Changes of direction, from one axis to another, are marked by two existing buildings, the Hassan II Mosque and the Saint-Pierre Cathedral, and the proposed museum and archive building, whose plan and section respond to the new axes.

POSTSCRIPT

When Adjaye reuses spatial concepts and forms of construction, he adapts them to their new role and they take on different identities. A similar process informs his urban proposals. As we have seen, an approach employed in one place can be combined with a response to a different condition in a second, to make a proposal that is well-suited to a third. But these projects have many attributes other than the way in which they respond to their urban locations and what they say about the city. The public buildings, for example, make bold statements about the work of the institutions they represent, and their materiality and spatial qualities are widely appreciated. They are nonhierarchical and informal in organization, offering alternative pathways and a range of destinations. Public places that address the individual, their forward-looking scenarios are rooted firmly in the present. Anchoring his buildings in place may give them an air of monumentality, but that is the basis on which Adjaye is able to engage other issues.

14.   Adjaye Associates, *Nakawa Nagura Feasability Master Plan*, project report, 2013, n.pag.

ARCH

...TIONS

THE SOURCE
Liverpool, United Kingdom, 2012
With Doug Aitken

David Adjaye studied art before turning to architecture, and he was
a postgraduate architecture student at London's Royal College of
Art, where he developed lasting friendships with several artists.
His natural affinity with the concerns and practices of contemporary
art have informed aspects of his architectural method and play a part
in the collaborative projects and urban studies that are the subject
of this section.

As the sole principal in his office, Adjaye is directly
involved in all aspects of Adjaye Associates' work, which is only
possible by developing collaborative understandings with individuals
in far-flung locations. The installation projects are artistic
collaborations that represent an elevated form of this practice, taking
place in limited time frames with the shared intention of producing
work of a kind that neither participant would undertake individually.
In most cases, the relevant artworks already exist and the object of the
collaboration is to organize a visual event based on the manner of their
display. This involves selecting some aspect of the artwork as the basis
for designing a complete environment, in which spatial sequencing and
atmospheric lighting are the primary considerations. Adjaye brings a
range of architectural technologies to bear on this task but mutes their
expression, as they are secondary to the concept of the installation. A
similar attitude, to do with architecture playing a supportive role in
timely events, underpins much of Adjaye's other design work.

Although it has been presented as an architectural survey,
African Metropolitan Architecture, completed between 2000 and 2011,
is decidedly artistic in nature, especially in the procedures Adjaye
followed in collecting the material for the book. A survey would normally
involve a period of research and planning, but Adjaye's approach was to
record the cities as he encountered them on his visits. His photographs
reflect this experience, appearing to have been taken while constantly on
the move, and it is the uniquely personal quality of the images, rather
than any imposed structure, that provides continuity. The study was
well underway before there was any possibility of publishing it, and
the primary aim was to create a private photographic archive covering
the building types and development patterns of the continent's capital
cities. Adjaye first considered the six geographic terrains that
structure the book when material on ten of the cities was presented
in an exhibition. The terrains were introduced to provide a basis on
which to interpret the photographic material—the photographs were
not made to suggest specifications for each terrain. This distinction
characterizes the ways in which Adjaye uses the study to inform the
buildings that he is now designing in Africa.

An unexpected consequence of African Metropolitan
Architecture is that it provides an overview in which the physical
space between the capital cities has been omitted, and they appear
side by side. The Europolis study of 2008 envisages a situation where
something similar has happened in reality, and the major cities of
Europe have merged into a single conurbation. It was first presented at
an art biennial as a drawing in ocher-colored metallic foil mounted
between sheets of freestanding toughened glass, which could be viewed
from either side. Combining conditions that have previously existed
separately is a defining feature in several of Adjaye's recent projects.

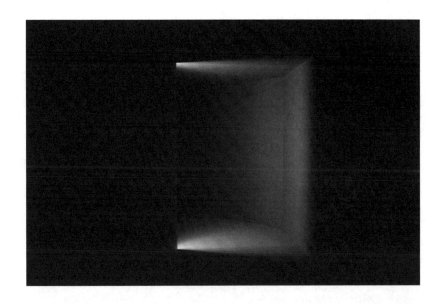

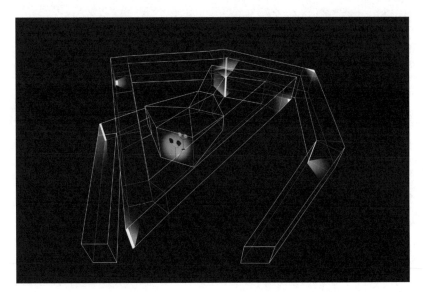

TURNING THE SEVENTH CORNER
Berlin, 2011
With Tim Noble and Sue Webster
One of the seven corners

Drawing showing route and display space

AMERICAN PRAYER
Paris, 2011
With Richard Prince
View of shingle-clad barn

Interior view of barn

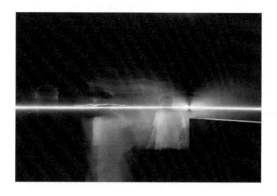

YOUR BLACK HORIZON
TBA21 Pavilion, Venice, Italy, 2005-06, and Lopud, Croatia, 2007
With Olafur Eliasson
Screen wall to entrance space

Interior view showing projection

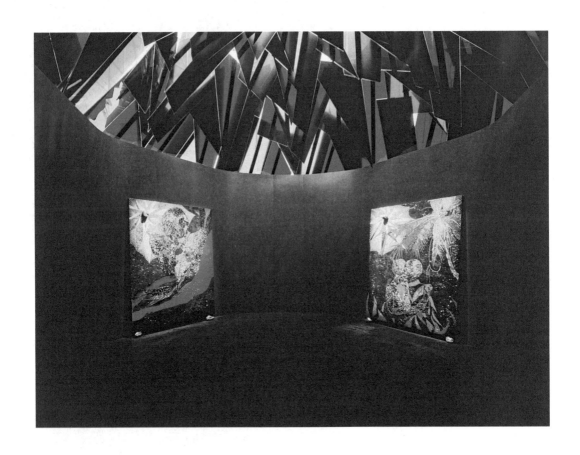

WITHIN REACH
Venice, Italy, 2003
With Chris Ofili
View showing glass ceiling and
Chris Ofili paintings

UPPER ROOM
London, 2002
With Chris Ofili
The room

Entrance passage

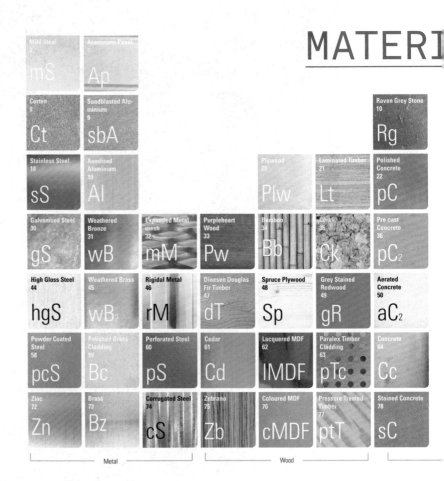

MATERI

The table, begun in 2006, places materials in groups,
reflecting their physical makeup, and orders them
according to their texture and appearance.
It provides the basis for a methodical approach to
the selection of materials.

TABLE

					Polyrey Plastic 1 **prP**	Polycarbonate 2 **Pl**
			Layered Crushed Glass 5 **lcG**	GRP 6 **Grp**	Recycled Plastic Panels 7 **rP**	
Black Stained Brick 11 **bB**	Terazzo 12 **Tz**	Felt 13 **Ft**	Coloured Glass Interlayer 14 **cG**	Back Painted Glass 15 **Bp**	Red Resin 16 **Rr**	Transluscent Polycarbonate 17 **tP**
Splitface Block 23 **Sb**	Stone 24 **St**	Polyester 25 **Py**	Grey Glass 26 **gG**	Transparent Glass 27 **tG**	Blue Rubber flooring 28 **Br**	Monopan 29 **Mp**
Grey Slate 37 **Gs**	Pebbles 38 **Ps**	Wool 39 **W**	Laminate Green Glass 40 **lgG**	Opaque Glass 41 **oG**	Green Rubber flooring 42 **Gr**	Rubber Mat 43 **Rm**
Sienna Slate 51 **sS$_2$**	Ceramic 52 **Ce**	Leather 53 **L**	Laminate Blue Glass 54 **lbG**	Translucent Glass 55 **tG$_2$**	Norament Rubber Flooring 56 **Nr**	Mastic Asphalt 57 **Ma**
Grey/Green slate 65 **gS$_2$**	Porcelian 66 **Pc**	Carpet 67 **Ca**	Laminated Clear Glass 68 **lcG**	Toughened Glass 69 **tG$_3$**	Black Rubber Flooring 70 **Ru**	Recycled Tortoise Shell 71 **Ts**
Stained Plaster 79 **sP**	Clay Tiles 80 **Cti**	Kvadrate Soft Cell 81 **Ksc**	Gradient Coloured Glass 82 **gcG**	Mirror Glass 83 **Mi**	Perspex 84 **Px**	PVDF Plastic 85 **PVDF**

Stone ⌐ Fabric ⌐ Glass ⌐ Plastic

Glass Panels by Chris Ofili 86 **Gco**	Resin Flooring 87 **Rf**	Aluminium Foam Laminated Glass 88 **Alg**	Aluminium Honeycomb 89 **Alh**	Fibre Reinforced Concrete 90 **Tc**	Wood Wool 91 **Ww**	Laminated Veneer Lumber 92 **lV**
Sand Resin 93 **Sr**	Aluminium & Resin 94 **Alr**	Crushed Glass Resin 95 **cG$_2$**	Zebrano Veneer 96 **Zv**	Wood Fibre board 97 **Wf**	Bear grass 98 **Bg**	Orientated Strandboard 99 **Osb**

Composite Materials

AFRICAN M
ARCHI

The Maghreb: Algiers, Algeria

ROPOLITAN
CTURE

Desert: Cairo, Egypt

The Sahel: Bamako, Mali

Forest: Yaoundé, Republic of Cameroon

Savanna and Grassland: Antananarivo, Madagascar

Mountain and Highveld: Asmara, Eritrea

EUR

Europe

Europolis

Europolis (2008) is an ideal city, the components of which
already exist. It weaves the physical and spatial infrastructure
of Europe's capital cities into a single system.

LIS

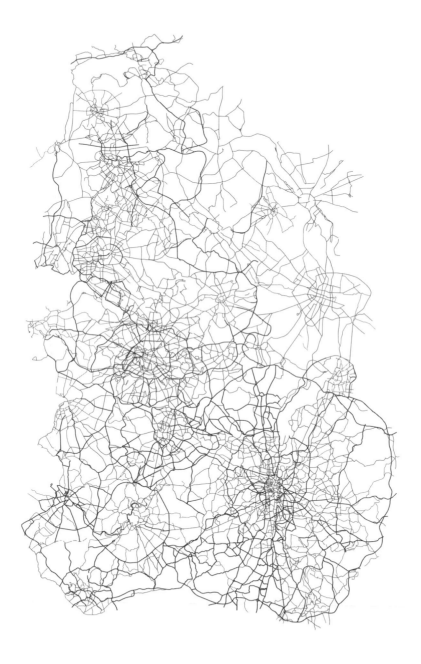

Main roads

The radial roads of the existing cities are subsumed
within a continuous network, providing increased choice and
freedom of movement.

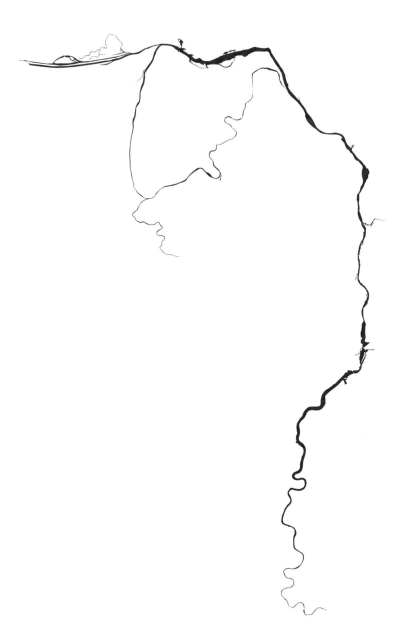

Waterways

As an alternative to the widely spaced rivers
that grace the continent, a single river incorporates
characteristic stretches from several of them.

Green spaces

A certain formality in the historic placement of open space is
replaced by a more informal distribution pattern, and residents are
able to access a greater variety of recreational spaces.

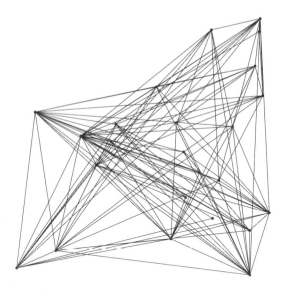

Flight paths

Despite a reduction in the overall area, compared
with Europe, the principal urban hubs are connected by air
and flight times are considerably reduced.

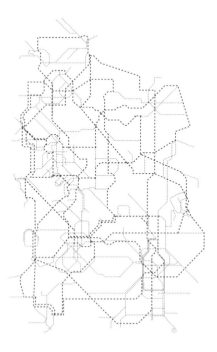

Metros

Both hubs and local centers are served by the unified
public transit system, which offers a combination of
express and local services to all destinations.

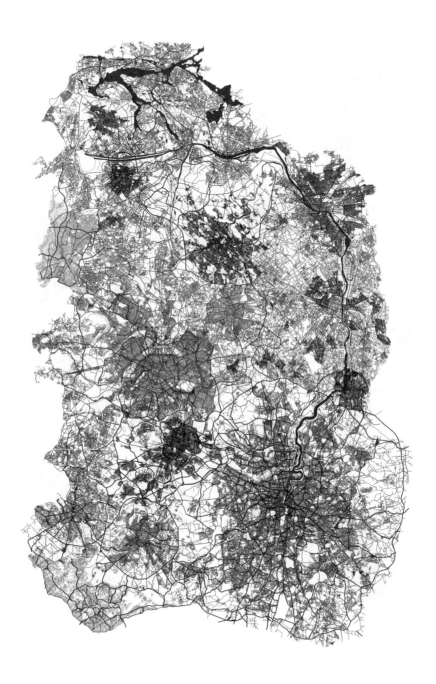

All systems

THE SOURCE
Liverpool, United Kingdom, 2012
With Doug Aitken
Detail of roof structure

OTHER
MONUMENTALITIES
MABEL O. WILSON

(Fig 01) Smithsonian Institution
Washington, D.C., c. 1855
Distant view (The Smithsonian
Institution is at upper left)

(Fig 02) NATIONAL MUSEUM OF AFRICAN
AMERICAN HISTORY AND CULTURE
Washington, D.C., 2009-16
Prototype facade, night view

(Fig 03) James Renwick Jr. (American, 1818–1895)
The Castle, Washington, D.C., 1847-55

As a profitable field of study and fitting point of departure, whence to reach an Architecture suited to our own country and our own time, the manner of the Smithsonian building supplies a valuable commentary ...

Robert Dale Owen, *Hints on Public Architecture* (1849)

To find architecture in the unending flow of the present is precisely to interrupt that flow. Forgetting the past inevitably means forgetting a particular past in favor of another, no matter how recent it might be. The modern monument is not a contradiction in terms. The monument is always modern.

Mark Wigley, *The Architectural Cult of Synchronization* (2000)

The Smithsonian Institution, founded in 1835, (Fig 01) took twenty years to be realized as a monument to the United States's commitment to the creation and dissemination of knowledge about what constitutes America and who is American. Its original ideological and scientific mission also positioned a distinct American culture as foundational for the public spaces emerging in and shaping the nation's capital. In his lengthy treatise *Hints on Public Architecture* (1846), congressional representative Robert Dale Owen wondered how the architecture of the Smithsonian might embody the nation's moral character, and how it might establish a unique national style representative of a modern society, one guided by the scientific and artistic advancements the new public institution would collect, study, and display. Owen concluded that the "certain conditions ... set down as essential, in any style of architecture that shall justly obtain, in our republic, the character of national" were that it be suited to the climate, utilitarian in nature, and affordable for the government of the still-young republic.[01]

By contrast, the Smithsonian's National Museum of African American History and Culture (NMAAHC), an idea first proposed in 1915 as the National Memorial Building in honor of black soldiers and sailors, will have taken one hundred years to open its doors.[02] (Fig 02) What might constitute an appropriate national style for a public institution was vociferously debated at the founding of the Smithsonian in the mid-nineteenth century, but is the subject still relevant today, as the Smithsonian completes the NMAAHC's construction on the National Mall and opens the new museum in 2016, a half-mile away from the original Smithsonian building, known as "The Castle"? (Fig 03) Designed by a team led by David Adjaye, the NMAAHC will realize Director Lonnie Bunch's vision that it "help all Americans remember, and by remembering, ... stimulate a

01.   Robert Owen, *Hints on Public Architecture: Containing, Among Other Illustrations, Views and Plans of the Smithsonian Institution: Together with an Appendix Relative to Building Materials* (G. P. Putnam, 1849), p. 8.

dialogue about race and help to foster a spirit of reconciliation and healing."[03] Bunch's project of critical memory plumbs the official history of the nation—a history shaped in part by the Smithsonian's nineteenth-century commitment to "progress." As a report made at the time of its founding states, the institution's mission was to "promote the discovery of new truths" among men.[04] Bunch's contemporary critical reflection posits "raciality" as a central thread in the formation of the nation's grand historical tapestry, woven from mythologies of exceptionalism and heroic representations of great deeds. Equally central to the new NMAAHC's mission will be emphasizing the centrality of African American contributions to United States history. To fulfill this aim, in what ways does Adjaye's new museum create the space for a "counterarchive" and present itself as a "countermonument" to the original Smithsonian's legacy as a nation-building project?

Moreover, if the Smithsonian's founding mission was to discover and represent the nation's cultural character, then why did it take so long for the cultural production of peoples of African descent to be fully incorporated into its collections and represented in its galleries? To answer that question it is important to discern how, in its quest for "the discovery of new truths," the Smithsonian cultivated a racialized national identity—one whose European cultural roots would always exclude from its address those who were not at the vanguard of Western civilization's advance, treating them instead as the object of research and display, as the focus of the gaze of the rational thinking subject—the scientist, the artist, the architect, and the American citizen. With its unique double-clad bronze-coated Corona wrapping its interior public galleries, how does Adjaye's building critically challenge and complicate the readings of identity, race, and culture implicit in how the nation was represented and imagined through the Smithsonian's original mission and structure?

RESEARCH, RACE, & THE NATION'S HISTORICAL ARCHIVE

To achieve the goal of building a formidable national institution dedicated to knowledge, the Smithsonian had to be planned in meticulous detail. In the mid-1840s its newly formed Board of Regents, a body composed of white politicians, educators, and scientists (including the vice president of the United States, the chief justice of the US Supreme Court, and the mayor of Washington, D.C.), conceived the Smithsonian's mission as focusing on three primary areas: the physical (the material world including man); the moral and political (the individual and the state); and literature and fine art (culture).[05] Through the collection of materials within these designated areas of research, the emerging scientific disciplines would examine the forces that transformed the conditions of the material world. In other words, learned men working in the field and in the

02. In 1915 a group of black citizens proposed but failed to get the US Congress to fund a national monument dedicated to the memory of black soldiers who had fought in the nation's many conflicts, in particular the Civil War. After a decade of lobbying, the proposed building—a Neoclassical temple designed by black architect Edward R. Williams—grew to include a library, museum, and auditorium, like the early Smithsonian. With a planned five-thousand-seat capacity, the hall needed to be large enough to accommodate events such as school graduations because, due to racism, Washington, D.C.'s black residents had limited access to large public venues elsewhere in the capital. Similar ideas for a national museum dedicated to black contributions were put forward by various groups in the late 1930s, mid-1960s, and early 1990s, but each time racist congressional representatives derailed the initiative, despite its enjoying support from sympathetic white politicians. See Mabel O. Wilson, *Negro Building: Black Americans in the World of Fairs and Museums* (University of California Press, 2012).

03. "About Us," National Museum of African American History and Culture, last modified Apr. 15, 2014, http://nmaahc.si.edu/about.

04. Smithsonian Institution, ed., *Tenth Annual Report of the Board of Regents of the Smithsonian Institution* (A. O. P. Nicholson, 1856), p. 7.

05. "Introduction," *Smithsonian Contributions to Knowledge* 1, 1 (1848), p. 5.

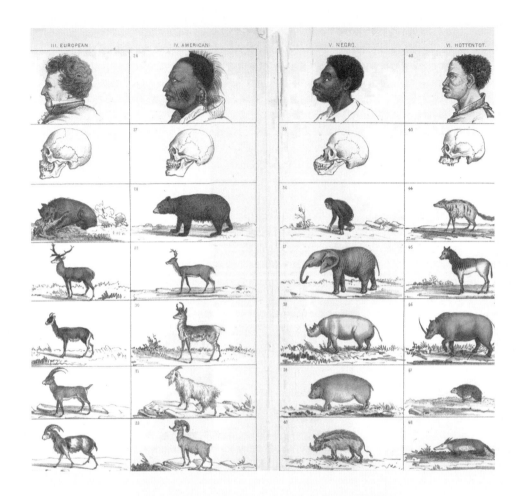

(Fig 04) Racial taxonomy published
in Josiah Nott and George Glidden,
Types of Mankind (J. B. Lippincott, 1854)

(Fig 05) Vertner Woodson Tandy and George Washington Foster
(American, 1885–1949 and 1886–1923)
The Temple of Beauty in the Great Court of Freedom, 1913,
published in *Crisis*, December 1913

Smithsonian's laboratories would study how the nation's rich flora and fauna, mineral deposits, human populations, and cultural productions had changed over time. Collectively, their Smithsonian-funded research, the outcomes of which would be displayed to the public in the institution's galleries, would demonstrate how far "American civilization," the culture that bound together its white population, had progressed. Scholar Andreas Huyssen has stated that "the main concern of nineteenth-century nation-states was to mobilize and monumentalize national and universal pasts so as to legitimize and give meaning to the presentation and to envision the future: culturally, politically, and socially."[06] The state's effort to cultivate a national spirit was a bid to galvanize the country at a moment when westward expansion and the creation of new states forced the issue of slavery onto the national agenda. Slavery would prove a divisive juridical question that would eventually split the republic into Northern and Southern adversaries. The monumentality of the Smithsonian served as a reminder not of the past but of the contemporary values of the nation precisely at a moment when the Union was under threat.

The nineteenth-century public museum, as scholar Tony Bennett has argued, arose alongside schools and libraries out of governments' need to mobilize forms of culture as new technologies of power. A multivalent exhibitionary social space, the modern public museum would not only proffer cultural representations to increase public knowledge about the nation, but it would also function as a sphere where the activities of those visitors granted entrance to the galleries could be cultivated, observed, and regulated according to new norms of public behavior.[07] The Smithsonian's founding mission deployed the "analytics of raciality," theorist Denise Ferreira da Silva's term for how the Enlightenment and Post-Enlightenment quest for the "truth of Man" in Europe (and the United States) produced and represented concepts of human difference that formed the foundations of racial science by the mid-nineteenth century. In her rigorous review of modern epistemology, Da Silva charted how the play of reason brought the modern thinking subject—in this case the American citizen—into representation in nineteenth-century history and science.[08] During the Enlightenment, the evidence of human difference revealed by repeated colonial encounters was used to rationally separate human existence into two camps: minds who think and bodies that labor. Methods of comparative analysis and taxonomies, first conceived by natural historians and philosophers, juxtaposed objects (including buildings) to discern differences in their nature and the universal laws governing their behavior. From their deductions about purportedly innate differences in temperament and physique, physiognomists, naturalists, and zoologists asserted a historical lineage for human differences that would eventually be classified as racial types. Nineteenth-century scientific studies represented "race" as a natural and commonsensical outcome of historical development. These emerging discourses transformed "race"—referring to collectives of blood relations—into "the racial"—a scientific concept of universal human difference. (Fig 04) Da Silva strategically linked

06.   Andreas Huyssen, *Present Pasts: Urban Palimpsests and the Politics of Memory*, Cultural Memory in the Present (Stanford University Press, 2003), p. 1.

07.   Tony Bennett, *The Birth of the Museum* (Routledge, 1995), pp. 19–24.

08.   Denise Ferreira da Silva, *Toward a Global Idea of Race*, Borderlines (University of Minnesota Press, 2007). For Da Silva an early articulation of this modern onto-epistemological formation can be found in René Descartes's statement "I think therefore I am." This self-determined and self-conscious subject was radically different from one governed by God will's or the will of a king or queen. The early writings of Carl Linnaeus; Georges-Louis Leclerc, Comte de Buffon; Johann Kaspar Lavater; Georges Cuvier; and other natural scientists who classified humans by mental (moral) capacity and physical difference according to climate, became foundational for the later writings of racial science by Pierre Paul Broca, Arthur de Gobineau, Josiah C. Nott, George Robins Gliddon, and others. See ibid., pp. 30–31.

09.   Ibid., p. xix.

racial subjection with global subjection to "demonstrate how the productive weapons of reason, the tools of history and science, institute both man and his others as global-historical beings."[09]

When these differences in mental and physical aptitude were placed into a developmental framework of world history and, more specifically, national history, they produced signifiers of human difference—"The European," "The American," The Negro," and "The Hottentot"—that confirmed which racial groups were civilized, and thus advancing culturally, and which were primitive, and thus frozen in time. These categories were also central to a narrative of "progress" that located humans in different epochs of mental (hence moral) capability and social and cultural development. From this analysis it was deduced that white Americans and their shared European ancestors would lead civilization forward, and Africans and Native Americans, with their innately inferior moral abilities and primitive cultures, would need guidance toward becoming civilized—if in fact that were at all achievable. Explorers and researchers who undertook Smithsonian-funded expeditions spatialized concepts of racial difference as they aggressively recorded, collected, and mapped both the domesticated landscape of the American nation and the untamed territory of its frontier—the latter subdued by violent military incursions into what maps labeled "Indian Country." Once the gathered artifacts, maps, drawings, photographs, and research logs were studied in the Smithsonian's laboratories on the upper floors of The Castle, the findings would be presented in displays of specimens and artifacts, along with, for example, taxonomic paintings of Native Americans hung in the building's public galleries. The parsing of racial difference and ideas about what constitutes civilization were circulated to the wider American public via the Smithsonian's publications, and this parsing determined who deserved the rights and privileges of citizenship and who did not. In short, in the nineteenth century concepts from the emerging sciences of man (such as anthropology) translated into political actions and symbolic representations.[10]

IN WHAT NATIONAL STYLE SHOULD WE BUILD?

Indiana congressman Robert Dale Owen, a member of the first Smithsonian Board of Regents, recommended that the new building depart from the Neoclassical and Greek Revival style of architecture that had dominated the first fifty years of construction in Washington, D.C. He boldly proposed that the Smithsonian needed a new style, a style reflective of the nation's future, in order to "supply to this New World an architecture of its own."[11] Owen reasoned architecture was an art of utility, thereby identifying a central tenet of emerging modernism. He suggested what he called the Norman style (a revival that merged late Romanesque and early Gothic elements), which he believed represented a more defined, purer development of structure and form. The Romanesque's prosaic and practical merger of structure, form, and material would indicate that American genius, "piloted by good taste and steering by the polar star utility, may win honor and profit by a successful voyage into unexplored regions of art."[12] The Greek

---

10.   Ibid., p. 116.

11.   Owen was the son of Robert Owen, a Welshman who owned textile factories in Scotland and immigrated to America in 1825 to found New Harmony, a utopian socialist experiment on the plains of Indiana. The senior Owen envisioned an architecturally ambitious structure designed by Stillman Whitwell that would organize life in the settlement, where property was communally owned. The junior Owen, who opposed slavery and supported women's rights, worked with his father to establish a community that espoused equality and used education (a particular form based on a pedagogical movement called Pestallozianism) as a collective force to raise the mental and material conditions of the each member of the group. See Owen, *Hints on Public Architecture*, p. 11. See also Kathleen Curran, *The Romanesque Revival* (Pennsylvania State University Press, 2003).

12.   Owen, *Hints on Public Architecture*, p. 71.

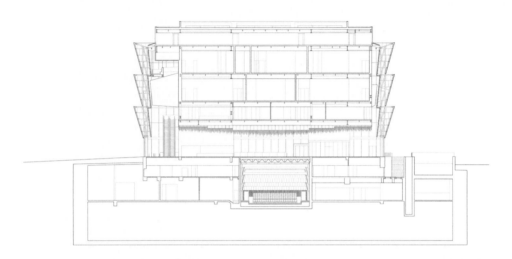

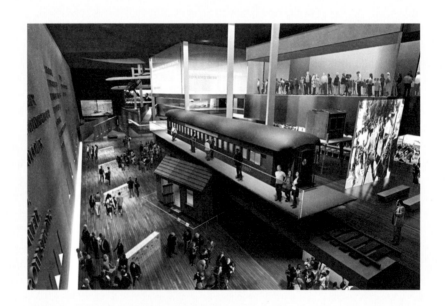

(Fig 06) NATIONAL MUSEUM OF AFRICAN
AMERICAN HISTORY AND CULTURE
Washington, D.C., 2009-16
Section

(Fig 07) NATIONAL MUSEUM OF AFRICAN
AMERICAN HISTORY AND CULTURE
Washington, D.C., 2009-16
Triple-height history gallery, rendering

Revival style utilized techniques of construction and materials (such as the post and lintel) suited to warmer Mediterranean climates, whereas the arcuated Romanesque could be understood as a uniquely Northern European style adapted to the climates and cultures of Germany and England—and the United States. Style, Owen implicitly argued, should be rooted to a race of people in a particular place at a specific time.

Leaving aside the pragmatics of how to build it, the Romanesque would represent America as an enlightened culture. This emerging American spirit was no longer colonial (that is, coarse and unrefined) but consistent with European aesthetic values of "truth" and "beauty," which elevated an implicitly racialized American culture. As Da Silva asserted, "the white ('Anglo Saxon') body, the body housing the U.S. American mind" became "an expression of European consciousness."[13] This meant that by the mid-nineteenth century, Greek culture—the origin of Neoclassicism—was, despite its cultural achievements, perceived as far too Mediterranean and, by proximity and cross-cultural exchange with Egypt, also too African.[14] Owen was not alone in arguing that the architecture of the "indolent" Egyptians was inferior. [15] Others were far more explicit about how race and architectural style were related. Historian Charles Davis has shown that during this period German, French, and American architects looked to the sciences of race, particularly ethnology, because they provided evidence of the superiority of particular architectural styles such as the Gothic.[16] Once completed by architect James Renwick, The Castle's fine wide arches, vaulted ceilings, and crenellated turrets that tower over the National Mall presented a proper national style, a monument that affirmed America's cultural legacy and announced its promising future.

The discourse of cultural progress exemplified by the Smithsonian's building asserted that the mentally and physically more advanced white, Northern European races would lead civilization forward. The darker races, mentally deficient and physically best suited for manual work, would be useful for their labor or, if necessary, could be eradicated through violence. Since the Smithsonian was erected in Washington, D.C., where slaveholding was still permitted, enslaved men were most likely employed during various stages of the building's construction, as they had been for the construction of the White House, the US Capitol, and other civic buildings.[17] Enslaved workers quarried and milled the red sandstone from nearby Montgomery County that was used to erect The Castle.[18] The productive dynamics of visible/invisible black bodies in the streets of Washington, D.C., and inside the halls of the nation's civic buildings was necessary for the conceptualization and material survival of the white subject that was the American citizen. How then can a new museum devoted to black history and culture be incorporated into an institution whose founding philosophy overwhelmingly excluded it? Does Adjaye's NMAAHC, with its shimmering bronze Corona inspired by African and African American sensibilities of material and form, adapt Owen's call for an institution "suited to our own country and our own time," by crafting a different language of representation than the Euro-American one employed in The Castle?

13.   Da Silva, *Toward a Global Idea of Race*, p. 201.

14.   The popularity of Neoclassicism in the late eighteenth century was in part prompted by the excavation of Roman and Greek ruins by practitioners of the emerging science of archaeology, as well as by colonial enterprises in Africa and Middle East. As art historian David Bindman has observed, once fully formulated as the Aryan model in the nineteenth century this theory (promoted a century earlier by Johann Winckelmann—the patriarch of art history)—turns "Greeks into an Indo-European people rather than an African one." The ancient model had attributed the originsn of Greek civilization to Phoenicians and Egyptians. Bindman explains that "this brought aesthetics into the service of race by denigrating the Egyptians as ugly and lacking the ability to have great thoughts." David Bindman, *Ape to Apollo: Aesthetics and the Idea of Race in the 18th Century*, Picturing History Series (Cornell University Press, 2002), p. 16.

15.   Owen, *Hints on Public Architecture*, p. 2.

COUNTERMONUMENTALITY

The NMAAHC joins the Smithsonian's constellation of eighteen museums and research facilities. While some might see it as an autonomous entity dedicated to the collection and display of African American history and culture, Adjaye insightfully understands that the new museum resides within an existing institutional context of national collections. He also recognizes that the new building occupies the overdetermined terrain of the National Mall, where the Smithsonian's branches, including the National Galleries of Art, American History, Air and Space, and Natural History, define the symbolic axis between the stately US Capitol building and the obelisk of the Washington Monument. As an archive of national patrimony that promoted white racial superiority, the Smithsonian at its inception deliberately disregarded the contributions that peoples of African descent made to the formation and expansion of the nation. In response to that legacy, the NMAAHC's mission will be to engage cultural memory to "help all Americans remember," to enunciate what had been silenced when the Smithsonian's national archive was selectively assembled. This suggests that the national history archive is no longer the powerful mise-en-scène of modernity that it once was.[19] A counterarchive like the NMAAHC will become what Huyssen describes as a "memory archive" and an active place "to imagine the future and to regain a strong temporal and spatial grounding of life and the imagination."[20] Adjaye's new museum also mobilizes memory to craft a countermonument, an other monumentality that counteracts the tendency for memorials and monuments to incite forgetting rather than remembrance in the present.[21]

Prior to the formation of the NMAAHC, black Americans had created various forms of counterarchives to the national institutions that refused to grant them status as modern subjects and citizens. In 1913 activist and sociologist W. E. B. Du Bois, for example, commissioned black architects Vertner W. Tandy and George W. Foster to design a neo-Egyptian style pavilion—the Temple of Beauty—for New York City's National Emancipation Exposition, a ten-day exposition celebrating the fiftieth anniversary of liberation from slavery.(Fig 05) The pavilion sat within the Twelfth Regiment Armory, a large hall located in the San Juan Hill neighborhood on Manhattan's West Side. As a counterarchive, the pavilion, which was embellished with hieroglyphics and Egyptian detailing, housed artworks that recounted African Americans' survival of enslavement with dignity, their heroic role in defending the nation, and their other contributions to US history and prosperity. Du Bois used the Temple of Beauty as a backdrop for his sweeping Pan-African pageant *The Star of Ethiopia*, which narrated a visual history of black achievements in both

16.   In his writings, nineteenth-century German architect Gottfried Semper claimed the evolution of architectural forms, for example, paralleled the evolution of racial variation. French architect Eugène Viollet-le-Duc developed a theory of Aryan migration out of India into Europe to legitimate, rationalize, and elevate European construction techniques over those of other, purportedly culturally inferior architectures. See Charles L. Davis, "Viollet-Le-Duc and the Body: The Metaphorical Integrations of Race and Style in Structural Rationalism," *arq: Architectural Research Quarterly* 14, 4 (2010), pp. 341–48; and Davis, "The Racial Epistemology of the Semperian Construction" (unpublished manuscript, 2013). Also see Darell Wayne Fields's seminal book *Architecture in Black* (Athlone Press, 2000).

17.   William C. Allen, "History of Slave Laborers in the Construction of the United States Capitol," June 1, 2005, "Art, Artifacts, and Architecture," Office of the Clerk of the US House of Representatives, http://artandhistory.house.gov/art_artifacts/slave_labor_reportl.pdf.

18.   Historian Mark Auslander's meticulous documentation has shown that several of the men who worked the Maryland quarry were descendants of men and women owned by President George Washington on his plantation, Mount Vernon. See Mark Auslander, "Enslaved Labor and Building the Smithsonian: Reading the Stones," *Southern Spaces*, Dec. 12, 2012, http://www.southernspaces.org/2012/enslaved-labor-and-building-smithsonian-reading-stones.

19.   Huyssen, *Present Pasts: Urban Palimpsests and the Politics of Memory*, p. 1.

20.   Ibid., p. 6.

21.   James Young, *At Memory's Edge: After-Images of the Holocaust in Contemporary Art and Architecture* (Yale University Press, 2000), p. 96.

(Fig 08) NATIONAL MUSEUM OF AFRICAN
AMERICAN HISTORY AND CULTURE
Washington, D.C., 2009–16
Contemplative Court, rendering

(Fig 09) NATIONAL MUSEUM OF AFRICAN
AMERICAN HISTORY AND CULTURE
Washington, D.C., 2009–16
South Porch with Washington Monument on left, rendering

(Fig 10) NATIONAL MUSEUM OF AFRICAN
AMERICAN HISTORY AND CULTURE
Washington, D.C., 2009-16
Central Hall, rendering

American and world history. Intent on correcting the perception that black Americans had no history worth representing, Du Bois's spectacle of one thousand performers narrated the long and auspicious history of peoples of African descent—a history that began long before emancipation. Critical of the limits that American nationalism had imposed on blacks, thereby impeding racial progress, Du Bois proposed a robust Pan-African solidarity as an alternative space of national belonging. Like Negro Buildings and events at previous Emancipation Expositions, the Temple of Beauty and *The Star of Ethiopia* aimed to inform the black counterpublic sphere and the dominant white mainstream public that black Americans had progressed since enslavement, thus recounting a history not represented in mainstream museums or expositions.[22] As a tactical political space, the Emancipation Exposition's counterarchive presented evidence of black advancement that attempted to reinstate the social equality and civil rights that the brutality of Jim Crow had drastically curtailed. But equally significantly, Du Bois's selection of a neo-Egyptian aesthetic posited an alternative, African, origin for world architecture, an alternative to the Euro-American Neoclassicism that dominated American civic architecture and had even been used for earlier Negro Buildings.

These nineteenth- and twentieth-century counterarchives created by black Americans— spaces that were temporary due to segregation's unrelenting regulating force—laid the foundation for the permanent museums dedicated to African American history and culture that began to spring up in the 1960s and will now include the NMAAHC. For the new museum's interior, Adjaye deployed a spatial strategy of nested boxes akin to the situating of Du Bois's Temple of Beauty within the larger armory building in New York. Adjaye earlier experimented with this Russian doll strategy in his design for the <u>Museum of Contemporary Art Denver</u>. Peeling back the NMAAHC's layers, the bronze-coated cast aluminum screen of the Corona forms the outer cladding and a glass curtain wall encloses the museum's interior.(Fig 06) Adjaye nested the triple-height history gallery, (Fig 07) the culture galleries, the theater, and other spaces where the public interacts with exhibitions and attends events at concourse level, below grade. Among the enfilade of galleries, the water- and light-filled void of the Contemplative Court offers a contrapuntal moment of stasis, a quiet interlude for reflection.(Fig 08) The galleries for temporary exhibitions are located on the third and fourth floors, behind the Corona.

On the ground floor, the Central Hall was conceived as an urban space where people could gather, and as the interface between the Concourse and the Corona. Because the structure of the entire building is carried by four widely spaced towers, it is a column-free space, with a dominant north-south axis connecting the South Porch with the oculus of the Contemplative Court, and an east-west axis marking the position of the escalators. The ceiling consists of a forest of suspended timbers whose ends describe a continuous curve, gradually dropping toward the center of the space. This plane forms a textured underbelly to the public galleries ensconced on the upper levels. Adjaye previously incorporated this gesture of the curved ceiling in <u>Nanjing House</u>, located in a remote neighborhood outside of Nanjing, China. In that project, three curved concrete planes draw light from above into a long living space. The curved planes contain the bedrooms, and, bulging downward, they compress the section, drawing the exterior to the interior. The NMAAHC ceiling exponentially expands the scale of the curved volumes, as it sweeps upward from the center toward the museum's perimeter.(Fig 10) This gesture pulls the exterior public

22.   Wilson, *Negro Building*, pp. 149–60.

cladding of the Corona to meet the interior surfaces of the museum's galleries. "Architecture and the interior enfold around one another," as theorist Sylvia Lavin has said of the autonomous interiors of contemporary buildings, "to produce the ever surprising and still new experience of the perceptually new and experientially singular."[23] At the NMAAHC the interior public spaces for the performance of collective memory that rewrites national history enfolds to meet the public space of the National Mall, which in turn projects alternative and evolving national identities—an encounter that will always create "the perceptually new."

Within the institutional network of the Smithsonian, one that has been 150 years in the making, Adjaye's NMAAHC, particularly its exterior presence, challenges the established conventions of national architectural style and meaning. The Castle's red sandstone and Romanesque detailing, which rationalized the museum's scientific and public functions as a structural tectonic, were, at the time of its founding, a radical break from the established Neoclassical aesthetic for civic building. But Owen's quest to ground an authentically American national style in the Romanesque failed to gain popularity. Instead the form and materials of Neoclassicism persisted in all genres of civic architecture well into the twentieth century. A survey of many of the Smithsonian's museum buildings shows how the marble temple of the National Gallery of Art's West Building (1941), designed by John Russell Pope, and the abstract classicism of the National Museum of American History (1961), designed by McKim, Mead & White, for example, echo the Greek Revivalism of the iconic halls of government such as the White House and US Capitol. Although the acute triangular volumes of I. M. Pei's modernist East Building for the National Gallery of Art (1981) boldly break from the rectangular temple forms of the neighboring parts of the museum, the building is clad in the same pink Tennessee marble of Pope's West Building. On the south side of the Mall, Skidmore, Owings & Merrill's chief architect Gordon Bunshaft wrapped the hulking cylinder of the Hirshhorn Museum in precast concrete panels fabricated from an aggregate of pink granite, thus giving its spare modernist volume a monumental appearance comparable to that of the other museums lining the National Mall corridor. "The perfect material is stone," wrote architect and theorist Mark Wigley, "natural but frozen, organic but still, petrified life. The cult of monumentality is intimately tied to that of stone."[24] The marble and granite claddings mark loss as well as longevity—and thus serve their monumentalizing function of representing enduring American cultural values.

Adjaye designed the exterior of the NMAAHC's Corona—a double cladding composed of an outer screen of bronze-coated cast aluminum panels over a glass curtain wall—to dematerialize the massive white stone volumes of the Smithsonian museum typology. The bronze coating of the screen references the cast- and wrought-iron gates, balconies, and other objects crafted by enslaved and freed blacksmiths in the antebellum South, especially the Carolina Lowcountry and the bayous around New Orleans. Adjaye abstracted the historical screens' organic filigree into a geometric pattern whose lines can be modulated depending on how much light needs to be filtered. The cant of the Corona's tiers echoes the seventeen-degree angle of the pyramid capstone of the nearby Washington Monument, whose spare, angular Egyptian aesthetic is unique within the Mall precinct. The coursing pattern of the bronze screen also mimics the placement of the Washington Monument's large marble stones. (Fig 09) These references to Africa and Africanisms in American cultural traditions are relevant to the museum's story. While it is compelling to delve into what

23.   Sylvia Lavin, *Kissing Architecture* (Princeton University Press), p. 69.

24.   Mark A. Wigley, "The Architectural Cult of Synchronization," *October*, no. 94 (Fall 2000), p. 37.

(Fig 11) FRANCIS A. GREGORY LIBRARY
Washington, D.C., 2008-12
Interior view showing position of staircase

(Fig 12) IDEA STORE CHRISP STREET
London, 2002-04
Front facade

(Fig 13) RIVINGTON PLACE
London, 2003-07
Street view

these cultural references symbolize, it is more productive to consider how Adjaye arrived at and deployed their operative techniques. The thickened layer of exterior cladding, for example, is a technique that he developed in earlier projects such as London's two Idea Stores (Fig 12) and Rivington Place. (Fig 13) Ashanti kente cloths (in the former) and a Sierra Leonean Sowei mask (in the latter) inspired the repetition and modularity of geometric forms that facilitate the shifting, stretching, and compression of patterns that compose the facades' surfaces.[25] The thickening of the facade reaches a new level of plastic expression in the diamond curtain wall of the Francis A. Gregory Library, near the NMAAHC. Internally, panels of Douglas fir plywood expand the thickness of the glass curtain wall to create a playful solid/void diamond pattern that, like a textile, stretches around the library's four facades. (Fig 11) The same pattern is employed in the structure of the glass ceiling and the structural steelwork of the roof. In all of these projects, the facade becomes a dynamic skin that wraps the volumes and spaces organizing the interior functions.

Adjaye delaminated the upper sections of the NMAAHC's facade into two entities: one bronze-coated cast aluminum (ornamental) and the other glass (structural). The visible bronze-colored filigree screen hovers above the ground, signaling that it does not support the building's load and challenging the stability that characterizes the structures on the National Mall. Following the same principle that Gottfried Semper observed in a Caribbean hut displayed at the Great Exhibition in London in 1851, the panelized Corona is suspended from above, and its openings dissolve the density of the bronze to reveal the public spaces behind.[26] Visually the Corona subverts the classical tripartite division of base, middle, and cornice that organizes the other nearby Smithsonian buildings. Adjacent to the massive white marble edifices that rise atop their grand stepped bases, the bronze surface of the Corona shimmers in the daylight as it delicately floats above the landscape; at night, illuminated from inside, it exposes the interior volumes. The NMAAHC's doubled veil destabilizes the monumental language of the Smithsonian museum type. The representation of an enduring unified national identity is no longer solid and sturdy but dematerializes before our very eyes; it awaits an active redefinition from the fragments of knowledge about African American contributions to national and world history that we gain within the spaces of the museum's counterarchive. (Fig 14)

The new NMAAHC building both challenges and amends the racialized representations of national identity that haunt Washington, D.C., from the US Capitol to the Lincoln Memorial. From inside its galleries visitors will reimagine the American mythos of liberty and freedom as they gaze out across the capital city's symbolic landscape—one fraught with its own history of slavery and segregation, now made visible by Adjaye's intervention. The NMAAHC will be a museum not only "suited to our own country and our own time," but more importantly, with its African American and African sensibilities, it forms a living monument built for our complex, interconnected world.

25. David Adjaye, Peter Allison, Okwui Enwezor, et al., *Making Public Buildings: Specificity, Customization, Imbrication* (Whitechapel Gallery/Thames and Hudson, 2006), pp. 46–55.

26. Gottfried Semper, *Style: Style in the Technical and Tectonic Arts; or, Practical Aesthetics*, trans. Harry Francis Mallgrave and Michael Robinson (Getty Publications, 2004), p. 666.

(Fig 14) NATIONAL MUSEUM OF AFRICAN
AMERICAN HISTORY AND CULTURE
Washington, D.C., 2009–16
Theater, rendering

LIST OF PROJECTS

SMALL MONUMENTS

PAVILIONS

SHADA
London, 1999,
with Henna Nadeem

At the heart of a refurbished housing development in London's East End, a disc of Corten steel, supported on a cluster of columns, makes a protected meeting space. The steel umbrella has laser-cut perforations that reproduce the shadow pattern cast by the leaves of London's ubiquitous plane trees, and the columns support small seats and tables.

ASYMMETRIC CHAMBER
Manchester, United Kingdom,
2003, and New York, 2005, with
soundtrack by Peter Adjaye

With its linear organization, this pavilion prefigures the arcade-like spaces in some of Adjaye's public buildings. The walls incorporate closely spaced frames of recycled timber, which are exposed in the two side spaces and lined with plywood in the central space. The only lighting in the pavilion is at floor level.

LENGTH x WIDTH
x HEIGHT
London, 2004, with
soundtrack by Charlie Dark
and Indie Choudhury

With the same alignment as Rivington Place (the building that would eventually occupy this location) a tilted tubular structure explores the experience of moving from one end of the site to the other. The construction follows a similar pattern to that of Asymmetric Chamber, with the addition of rhythmically placed translucent panels.

HORIZON
London, 2007, and Rome, 2008

This is the first example of the screen-like construction employed in many of the later pavilions. The plan is based on two triangles; where they intersect, a dimly lit threshold leads to a viewing gallery, whose splayed walls frame a backlit image of the Sea of Galilee.

SCLERA
London, 2008

Standing within sight of the London Eye, the spatial concept for Sclera is based on the human eye and its role in visual perception. Closely packed frames of tulipwood form an oval enclosure, with parts of some frames omitted to make external openings and a complex suspended ceiling.

SPECERE
Kielder Water and Forest Park,
United Kingdom, 2009

Conceived both as a viewing platform and a shelter for walkers and cyclists, this pavilion is located at the summit of Deadwater Fell, close to the Anglo-Scottish border. The slatted construction is closely packed in the direction of the prevailing wind and open toward the view.

GENESIS
Miami, 2011

Compared to Horizon, in which two triangular volumes are superimposed, the central space of this pavilion is formed by subtracting an ovoid volume from a triangular volume. Where the ovoid breaks through the walls and roof of the timber structure, four openings are created: an entrance and an exit, a window, and a distorted oculus.

EPHEMEROPTERAE
Vienna, 2012

Combining a small stage and a proscenium arch in one continuous structure, Ephemeropterae hosts a program of lectures and performances organized by Thyssen-Bornemisza Art Contemporary (TBA21) in the Augarten, a Baroque park. The overall volume is tapered in plan and section, distancing or foreshortening the view of the park.

RIVER READING ROOM
Gwangju, South Korea, 2013

Four concrete piers indented with bookshelves support a timber roof above a public staircase, which connects street level to a riverside park. The piers are designed to withstand seasonal flooding. At other times, the space around the staircase is serviced by the city library and used as an outdoor reading room.

THE CHAPEL
Chicago, 2015

Crossing the line from temporary to permanent structure, the pavilion encloses an emphatic acoustic space for performances and debate on the city's South Side. The solid/void strategy is directly comparable to that of Genesis, except that the triangular volume has been placed in an upright position to produce a snow-discharging roof, which was not necessary in Miami.

DESIGN

MONOFORMS
London, 2007

Inspired by desert landscapes and the rock architecture of Petra, Jordan, Monoforms is an open-ended furniture system based on a language of form, rather than on technical detail. The visual properties of each piece suggest how it might sit within a larger environment, like a building in a landscape or city.

STAR COLLECTION
Milan, 2012

As with Adjaye's buildings, the materiality of these vases is immediately engaging, and due to their geometry they sit comfortably in a variety of settings. Handmade in copper, they are lined with black crystals.

THE WASHINGTON COLLECTION
2013, for Knoll, New York

Developed while Adjaye was working on the National Museum of African American History and Culture, these designs reflect his interest in shell and frame structures—in this case in connection with the human body. The structural ribs follow the stress lines in the chairs, and the intersections between the curved volumes give stiffness to the table.

LIVING SPACES

ELEKTRA HOUSE
London, 1998–2000

Adjaye's first building includes several elements that he went on to develop in later projects: a table-like structure, from which the external walls are suspended; an upper floor set within a larger enclosure, suggesting a building within a building; and an extended circulation route that follows the perimeter. The ground floor doubles as a family room and art space.

DIRTY HOUSE
London, 2001–02

This is the first of several London houses in which the shell of an older building is colonized by a new structure. Here, a small factory has been converted to studio use and the patched-up walls have been unified by the application of an anti-graffiti coating. The artist clients live on the top floor, where a light steel frame supports a cantilevered roof.

LOST HOUSE
London, 2002–04

Within an older mixed-use building, what was once an access road has been roofed over to become the main living space, while the bedrooms and a lap pool occupy a raised platform previously used for deliveries. The structural enclosure of the living area employs closely spaced timber arches, and natural light is admitted by three courtyards.

PITCH BLACK
New York, 2003-06

Establishing a precedent for Adjaye's buildings in Denver, Colorado, Pitch Black develops a robust section within a skin-like enclosure that transforms itself into a canopy on the rear facade. Designed for two artists, the studio spaces are separated from the outside world by a four-story lobby, and their geometry is closely matched to each person's work.

SUNKEN HOUSE
London, 2003-07

Sunken House is similar in volume to its neighbors but is freestanding rather than semidetached. Constructed of prefabricated solid-timber panels with black-stained cladding, the kitchen and dining area are below ground level. A top-floor living space overlooks nearby gardens without intruding on their privacy.

LN HOUSE
Denver, Colorado, 2005-07

Standing end-on to the street, the exterior of this timber-framed house is clad in Corten steel. The organization of the section is a response to the lifestyle of the clients and the display requirements of their diverse art collection. These concerns intersect in a different fashion on each floor, where the choice of materials depends on the type of art displayed.

SILVERLIGHT
London, 2002-09

Occupying a strip of land between a busy road and a canal, the spaces within a steel frame are lined with a wide range of materials, creating a rich and varied interior. The main staircase connects the entrance to the top-floor living space and protects the interior from traffic noise.

SEVEN
New York, 2004-10

The section is a response to the permissible building volume and the need to bring natural light deep into the site. Designed for an art collector and his family, the primary spaces are an art gallery at street level and a salon above. Separated by a fountain court, the more private spaces are located in the rear.

NANJING HOUSE
Nanjing, China, 2004-12

Designed for a building exposition, the interior of this house is organized as an architectural landscape. Except for the entrance lobby, the ground floor is a continuous top-lit space whose ceiling height rises and falls due to the curved bedroom pods suspended from the roof. The external walls are clad in broken slate.

ASEM PA, MAKE IT RIGHT
New Orleans, 2007-11

Designed for the Make it Right Foundation as part of the program to rebuild the Lower Ninth Ward after Hurricane Katrina, these houses stand above ground level to escape future flooding. The porches found in older houses are replaced by an "urban room" at roof level, which is open to the breeze and the surrounding views.

NKRON
Ghana, 2008-12

Nkron is located on a site in the Forest zone, one of six geographic terrains Adjaye identified in his research project African Metropolitan Architecture. This zone has high humidity and heavy rainfall; indeed, the site is being developed as a tropical garden. The main elements of the brief are housed in a series of linked pavilions, whose raised floors and projecting roofs channel air movement and protect the external walls from direct sunlight and tropical downpours.

CASE STUDY HOUSING
IBA (International Building
Exhibition), Hamburg, Germany,
2010–13

A range of apartment types, each with an external space in the form of a loggia, have been assembled to form a compact urban block conceived as a prototype. For a low-carbon footprint, the construction employs a similar solid-timber system to that used in Sunken House.

HILL HOUSE
Port of Spain, Trinidad, 2008–14

The house is organized in three ascending steps. An entrance court and a gatehouse building are directly accessible from the road. A more formal entrance court and the main house, with a reception space for hanging large paintings, are located at the intermediate level. The back of the building addresses the top section of the site.

IN PROGRESS

ROMAN RIDGE GARDENS
Accra, Ghana, designed 2010

Similar in concept to Le Corbusier's Unité d'Habitation, individual apartments, surrounded by open space, are supported on a series of trays in a pigmented-concrete superstructure. The trays create shade and are open to the breeze; their tilted edges protect the balconies from rain, and the vegetation in the planters gives a sense of privacy.

MOLE HOUSE
London, designed 2013

This project is based on inserting a concrete structure in the shell of a derelict Victorian house on a triangular site in north London. Above the existing walls, the new structure supports a roof pavilion. At ground level, where the living spaces are located, the house begins to colonize the site.

DEMOCRACY OF KNOWLEDGE

IDEA STORE CHRISP STREET
London, 2002–04

The site consisted of an existing concrete deck above a row of shops on a postwar housing estate. The facade system employs structural lumber to brace a curtain wall whose light-responsive qualities complement the solidarity of the surrounding buildings. Internally, these fins support bookshelves, seating, and working surfaces.

IDEA STORE WHITECHAPEL
London, 2001–05

The Idea Stores are a concept pioneered by the London borough of Tower Hamlets to improve access to a wide range of information and educational facilities. To this end, the organization of the interior has the linear permeability of the street market at the foot of the building. All routes lead to a top-floor café, which affords views of the city.

NOBEL PEACE CENTER
Oslo, Norway, 2002–05

Within the walls of a bombed-out railway station, a sequence of scenographic interiors explores the history of the Peace Prize and its relevance to the contemporary world. Externally, a freestanding canopy directs visitors to the entrance and, in the other direction, frames a view of the Oslo town hall, where the Peace Prize is awarded.

BERNIE GRANT ARTS CENTRE
London, 2002–07

This project is intended to continue the life's work of the United Kingdom's first black member of parliament. It is arranged as a linear acropolis, with a major performance space at its heart, teaching spaces in the gateway building, and enterprise units in the linear building at the back of the site. The landscaped spaces make connections with the surrounding area.

RIVINGTON PLACE
London, 2003–07

Located in an area of workshops and studios, this compact building is shared by Iniva (Institute of International Visual Arts), a multicultural arts organization, and Autograph ABP, a black photographic agency. A three-story lobby provides access to the main public spaces: a gallery supported by both institutions, the Stuart Hall Library, and a public café.

STEPHEN LAWRENCE CENTRE
London, 2004–07

This institution commemorates Stephen Lawrence, a young black man who aspired to be an architect before his senseless murder. Offering courses and workshops relating to the built environment, the teaching spaces are located in two triangular pavilions whose oblique facades define an entrance court and address the surrounding landscape.

MUSEUM OF CONTEMPORARY ART
DENVER
Denver, Colorado, 2004–07

Based on the "building within a building" concept, the main galleries are arranged as freestanding volumes, surrounded by a circulation space. This arrangement allows the galleries to be used separately or in combination, depending on the exhibition program. Natural light is admitted through a system of skylights and filters through the double-skin external walls.

WAKEFIELD MARKET HALL
Wakefield, United Kingdom,
2005–08

Offering three types of retail space, the market is part of a wider development program, part of whose role is to facilitate connections in the surrounding area. The space for the external market performs a double function, as the roof forms a portico toward the bus station in one direction and frames a protected route to the city center in the other.

FRANCIS A. GREGORY LIBRARY
Washington, D.C., 2008–12

The singular form of this library addresses two contrasting conditions: a local highway and an area of mature woodland. Based on the shifting geometry of a cycad cone, the diagonal checkerboard pattern of the facades acts as a visual filter between interior and exterior, and the louvered roof reduces the impact of direct sunlight on the internal spaces.

WILLIAM O. LOCKRIDGE LIBRARY
Washington, D.C., 2008–12

With similar requirements to the Francis A. Gregory Library, this neighborhood library is located on a sloping site in a residential area. Toward the street the main volume is broken down into three pavilions whose scale is similar to that of the nearby houses. The pavilions house dedicated spaces for children, teens, and adults, and two of them define an informal entrance court.

NATIONAL MUSEUM OF AFRICAN
AMERICAN HISTORY AND CULTURE
Washington, D.C., 2009–16

The museum's permanent galleries are located at concourse level, below grade, and the temporary exhibition galleries are in the latticework-protected Corona, whose symmetry matches the classical frontality of other museums on the National Mall. A two-hundred-foot-long porch leads to the premier space in the building, the Central Hall: a new urban room for the city.

IN PROGRESS

MEMO—MASS EXTINCTION MEMORIAL
OBSERVATORY
Portland, United Kingdom,
designed 2009

All species declared extinct are represented by carved images on a continuous ramp, and the Robert Hooke Biodiversity Bell, standing on the floor of the main space, will ring with each new extinction. Built of Portland limestone, which is rich in fossils such as the Portland Screw that inspired the design, the memorial overlooks England's Jurassic Coast.

CAPE COAST SLAVERY MUSEUM
Cape Coast, Ghana, designed 2012

Cape Coast Castle, a slave fortress, is to be restored as an architectural monument and its historic contents rehoused in this new museum. The triangular form of the museum reflects the geometry of the castle, except that the new building hovers above a gathering space and its "lens windows" frame moments in Cape Coast's history, rather than looking out at attacks from the sea.

VARANASI SILKWEAVING FACILITY
Varanasi, India, designed 2013

On an open site next to the River Ganges, the plan reworks the bar arrangement seen in Nanjing House. Intended to put the city's traditional silkweaving on a sustainable footing, the building consists of a series of internal courts dedicated to the various stages of the weaving process, surrounded by an arcaded structure that stabilizes the environment in the work areas.

COLGATE CENTER FOR ART
AND CULTURE
Colgate University, Hamilton,
New York, designed 2014

The Longyear Museum of Anthropology and the Picker Art Gallery, currently in mixed-use campus buildings, will be combined with a community space at the heart of the village. Inspired by the mayor of Hamilton's residence with its central lantern, three pavilions adjust to the scale and position of nearby streets. The color of the precast concrete cladding refers to the adjacent buildings.

MUSEUM OF HISTORY,
ARTS AND CULTURE
Loango, Republic of the Congo,
designed 2014

Between the fifteenth and nineteenthth centuries, Loango was the site of an important precolonial state, which became wealthy due to trading in cloth, copper, and slaves. It gave its name to modern Angola. The museum will house a collection of tribal artifacts from this period.

URBAN SYSTEMS

MOSCOW SCHOOL OF MANAGEMENT
SKOLKOVO
Moscow, 2006–10

In response to the severity of the Russian winter, the main elements of the brief have been combined in a single structure. The disc element contains the teaching facilities, auditoriums, and a restaurant, and it protects the service area below. Its roof provides access to the Wellness Center, the Administration Tower, and the linear residential buildings. This arrangement minimizes the building's footprint and addresses the surrounding landscape.

PIETY BRIDGE & PIETY WHARF
New Orleans, 2008–14

Piety Bridge is one of the few places where the railway line running parallel to the Mississippi River can be crossed, giving access to a new park, to Piety Wharf, and to views of the river. Piety Wharf is a recreational deck enclosed by Corten steel walls, screens, and parapets, standing on the timber structure that supported the original wharf.

ALARA CONCEPT STORE
Lagos, Nigeria, 2011–14

In contrast to many of Lagos's shops and markets, this design store and consultancy is intended to be a destination in its own right. It will be joined by a boutique hotel, a gallery, and an office building to form a three-building cluster in landscaped grounds. The section of the store leads visitors to a roof-level gallery and terrace.

List of Projects

SUGAR HILL
New York, 2011–14

The program brings together affordable housing on the upper
floors and an early childhood center and the Sugar Hill Children's
Museum of Art and Storytelling in the podium. The building's
silhouette establishes its place in the city, and a landscaped public
plaza connects with the neighborhood. A rose pattern embossed in
the precast concrete panels recalls the area's bucolic past.

AÏSHTI FOUNDATION
Beirut, Lebanon, 2012–15

This project addresses several objectives. At the scale of the
city, it provides a landmark building that protects a landscaped
waterfront from a major highway and, in terms of function, it houses
a substantial retail volume and an art gallery. The latticework
facade is an environmental device and unifies the disparate components
of the brief.

IN PROGRESS

ELMINA COLLEGE
Elmina, Ghana, designed 2009

The teaching and communal facilities form a porous citadel on a
116-acre campus. Located in the Forest zone (one of six geographic
terrains Adjaye identified in his research project African
Metropolitan Architecture), a grid of large-scale arcades enclosing
landscaped courts mitigates the climatic conditions. This arrangement
provides choice and flexibility in relation to the detailed planning
of this area.

AL KAHRABA STREET
Doha, Qatar, designed 2010

Eight urban blocks have been laid out on both sides of Al Kahraba
Street to create a network of small courts and passageways leading
through the area. With retail space at street level and apartments
above, the project combines contemporary space standards and
technology with lessons learned from traditional Qatari architecture.
One block is devoted to office use.

CULTURAL CAMPUS FRANKFURT
Frankfurt, Germany, designed 2012

Nine of the city's cultural institutions are considering relocating
to a site where they will be able to share facilities such as
rehearsal spaces and restaurants. Framed by residential buildings,
the design concept is to create a city within a city: a single
development that includes, in a more abstract form, the basic
components of the existing city.

GOVERNMENT QUARTER MASTER PLAN
Libreville, Gabon, designed 2012

The master plan shows how government departments can be relocated
in close proximity to the one-time presidential palace, which is
now the seat of government rather than a residential site.
A new civic space links the government buildings to the city and
acknowledges the historic significance of the Saint-Pierre Cathedral
and the Hassan II Mosque.

ONE BERKELEY STREET
London, designed 2013

The brief required retail space, a hotel, and apartments on a site in
a protected historic area. Based on local precedents, the lower floors
reference nineteenth-century shopping arcades and the upper floors
reference eighteenth-century residential courts. The curved sections
of the facade are a response to the fluted columns and bay windows
found throughout the area.

HACKNEY FASHION HUB
London, designed 2013

Hackney is already the location of several designer outlet stores.
The proposal develops the current situation by utilizing the
spaces beneath a brick railway viaduct, and nearby sites, for
retail purposes. This extends the network of landscaped lanes that
characterizes the area.

ART CAMPUS TEL AVIV
Tel Aviv, Israel, designed 2013

The design concept is similar to Cultural Campus Frankfurt, except that it concerns one organization, Batsheva Dance Company, and relates to an actual site. In an area with few cultural facilities, the theater, performance studios, and support spaces cluster around a new urban square, in a porous arrangement that encourages use of the site and buildings.

HALLMARK TOWERS
Johannesburg, South Africa,
designed 2013

An existing building is to be stripped back to its concrete frame and reoccupied, with retail and commercial uses at street level, three floors of parking, a hotel, pool, and apartments. It is located in a mixed-use area of the city, close to the Maboneng Precinct, which is a center for the creative arts.

NAKAWA MASTER PLAN
Kampala, Uganda, designed 2013

The sixty-eight-acre site is a short distance from the city center and is bounded by a radial road and a railway line. Sections of the site will be developed according to their location, with a major landscaped space in a central position, employment and retail where they are most accessible, and residential areas that connect with the surrounding neighborhoods.

PETRONIA MASTER PLAN
Petronia, Ghana, designed 2013

Following on from African Metropolitan Architecture, Adjaye's study of African cities, this strategy for a new city is based on the use of development grids whose dimensions support different scales of building. Their position and orientation is a response to the undulating site and to landscape considerations. The circular area is the central business district and the small-scale grids are for residential purposes.

RESEARCH

INSTALLATIONS

UPPER ROOM
London, 2002,
with Chris Ofili

This installation consists of a suite of thirteen paintings by British artist Chris Ofili, and the chapel-like enclosure in which they are displayed, designed by Adjaye. The walls, floor, and ceiling are constructed of walnut-faced plywood whose scent is as subtle as its appearance.

WITHIN REACH
Venice, Italy, 2003,
with Chris Ofili

Selected to represent England at the Venice Biennale in 2003, Ofili invited Adjaye to transform the Neoclassical interior of the British Pavilion into a more suitable setting for his work. The spiral glass dome was based on discussions between them, and the surrounding spaces were painted red, green, and black.

YOUR BLACK HORIZON
TBA21 Pavilion, Venice, Italy,
2005-06, and Lopud, Croatia,
2007, with Olafur Eliasson

Your Black Horizon was a 360-degree light projection by Danish-Icelandic artist Olafur Eliasson. The pavilion was designed to enable viewers to access the space enclosed by the projection without casting shadows on it. A series of increasingly protected spaces led to the darkness of the main volume.

AMERICAN PRAYER
Paris, 2011,
with Richard Prince

Adjaye was responsible for the installation of an exhibition of American artist Richard Prince's collection of books and documents on American pop culture and counterculture, and related artworks, at the Bibliothèque Nationale de France. The centerpiece was a small barn clad in timber shingles taken from a similar structure in upstate New York, where some of the work was created.

TURNING THE SEVENTH CORNER
Berlin, 2011,
with Tim Noble and Sue Webster

A mysterious passage, dimly lit at each of seven corners, led to an irregular six-sided space in which a double-headed sculpture—made up of the gold-plated casts of rats, lizards, and bats, caught by the British artists' cat—was illuminated by a spotlight. The projected shadow showed the silhouette of the artists' heads back-to-back.

THE SOURCE
Liverpool, United Kingdom, 2012,
with Doug Aitken

This octagonal pavilion was designed to show twenty-four video interviews, conducted by American artist Doug Aitken, on the subject of creativity. It appeared at the Liverpool Biennial. Eight of the interviews could be projected at any one time. They could be viewed collectively or individually, by standing in the center of the space or moving into shallow bays on the external wall.

BUILDING FABRIC

MATERIAL TABLE
begun 2006

Like the periodic table in chemistry, Material Table locates materials in sequential groups according to their physical and tactile properties. For Adjaye, it is the basis for a measured approach to the selection of materials and the assessment of material effects. Samples of the materials are displayed in the same order in his office.

URBAN STUDIES

EUROPOLIS
Manifesta 7 European Biennial
of Contemporary Art,
Bolzano, Italy, 2008

In this study for an ideal city, the capital cities of Europe have been brought into closer proximity. The physical infrastructure of this hypothetical metropolis would be broadly similar to that of today, except that the distances between centers would be considerably reduced. Being brought closer to one another clarifies the nature of the cities' differences.

AFRICAN METROPOLITAN
ARCHITECTURE
2000–11

Adjaye's study explores the historical links between architecture and urbanism as demonstrated in Africa's capital cities. The cities were photographed over a ten-year period and the images have been the subject of several exhibitions and a publication (issued one year later). To clarify the impact of geography and culture, Adjaye grouped the cities into six geographic terrains.

Unless otherwise stated, all drawings, renderings, photographs, and model views of buildings by David Adjaye appear courtesy of Adjaye Associates.

Every effort has been made to contact and acknowledge copyright holders for all reproductions; additional rights holders are encouraged to contact the Art Institute of Chicago.

The following credits apply to all images in this catalogue for which separate acknowledgment is due.

ZOË RYAN, "WAYS OF BUILDING"
P. 21, fig. 01: Photograph by Lyndon Douglas. P. 22, fig. 02: Drawing by David Adjaye. P. 28, fig. 05: Photograph by Ed Sumner. P. 28, fig. 06: Photograph by Dean Kaufman. P. 33, fig. 07: Photograph by Ed Reeve. P. 34, fig. 08: Photograph by Konstantin Kokoshkin/Bloomberg via Getty Images. P. 34, fig. 09: Photograph by Fine Art Images/ Heritage Images/Getty Images; © 2014 Artists Rights Society (ARS), New York/VG Bild-Kunst, Bonn. P. 37, fig. 10: Photograph by Jeff Sauers. P. 38, fig. 12: Photograph by Ed Reeve.

"SMALL MONUMENTS"
P. 41: Photograph courtesy of Knoll. Pp. 44–45: Photographs by Kyungsub Shin. P. 46: Photograph by Jakob Polacsek. Pp. 48–49: 22 Group. P. 50: Photograph by Peter Sharpe. P. 51: Photograph by Leonardo Finotti. Pp. 52–54: Photographs by Ed Reeve. Pp. 55–56: Photographs by Lyndon Douglas. Pp. 58, 60: Photographs by Nussier Aicher.

DAVID ADJAYE, "THE LESSON OF AFRICA"
P. 61, fig 01; p. 62, fig. 02; p. 63, fig. 03; p. 66, fig. 04: Photographs by David Adjaye. P. 69, fig. 05: Photograph by Heini Schneebeli. P. 70, figs. 06, 07: Photographs by David Adjaye. P. 75, fig. 09; pp. 70–71, fig. 10; p. 78, fig. 11: Photographs by David Adjaye.

"LIVING SPACES"
Pp. 83–85: Photographs by Stephen Jameson. Pp. 86–87: Photographs by Lyndon Douglas. P. 88: Christian Lohfnik. Pp. 90–91: Photographs by Xia Zhi. P. 92 (top): Photograph by Robert Polidori. Pp. 92 (bottom), 94 (top): Photographs by Lyndon Douglas. P. 94 (bottom), 95: Photographs by Ed Reeve. Pp. 96–97: Photographs by Lyndon Douglas. Pp. 98–99: Photographs by Ed Reeve. P. 100: Photograph by Lyndon Douglas. P. 101: Photograph by Tod Eberle. Pp. 102–03: Photographs by Lyndon Douglas. P. 104 (top): Photograph by Ed Reeve. Pp. 104 (bottom), 105: Photographs by Lyndon Douglas. P. 106: Photograph by Ed Reeve. P. 107: Photographs by Lyndon Douglas. P. 112: Photograph by Stephen Jameson.

ANDREA PHILLIPS, "COSMOPOLITAN PLACE MAKING"
P. 113, fig. 01: Photograph by Ed Reeve. P. 114, fig. 02: Photograph by Lyndon Douglas. P. 115, fig. 03; p. 117, fig. 04; p. 120, fig. 05; pp. 122–23, fig. 06; p. 124, fig. 07; p. 126, fig. 08: Photographs by Ed Reeve.

"DEMOCRACY OF KNOWLEDGE"
Pp. 128–29: Photographs by Jeff Sauers. Pp. 131–32: Photographs by Edmund Sumner. P. 133 (top): Photograph by Jeff Sauers. P. 133 (bottom), pp. 134–35: Photographs by Edmund Sumner. Pp. 136–37: Photograph by Lyndon Douglas. Pp. 138–39: Photographs by Dean Kaufman. Pp. 140–41 (top): Photograph by Lyndon Douglas. P. 141 (bottom): Photograph by Edmund Sumner. Pp. 142–43, 144–45, 146: Photographs by Ed Reeve. P. 147: Photograph by Tim Soar. P. 148: Photograph by Ed Reeve. P. 149: Photograph by Tim Soar. Pp. 154–55: Photograph © Dorian Shy. P. 164: Photograph © 2014 Allen Russ/ Hoachlander Davis Photography, LLC.

OKWUI ENWEZOR, "GESTURES OF AFFILIATION"
P. 165, fig. 01; p. 166, fig. 02: Photograph by Lyndon Douglas. P. 171, fig. 03: Tim Soar. P. 180, fig. 08: The Washington Post/Getty Images. P. 183, fig. 09: The Bridgeman Art Library/Getty Images.

"URBAN SYSTEMS"
Pp. 189–90: Photograph by Iwan Baan. Pp. 191, 192–93: Photographs by Ed Reeve. Pp. 194–95: Photograph by Iwan Baan. Pp. 196–97: Photographs by Ed Reeve. Pp. 198–99: Photograph by Tim Hurseley. Pp. 200–01: Photographs by studio Hans Wilschut.

PETER ALLISON, "READING THE CITY"
P. 222, fig. 02: Photograph by Magali Moreau. P. 223, fig. 03: Photograph by Mike Kane. P. 229, fig. 06: Photograph by Peter Allison. P. 233, fig. 09: Photograph by Dan Borelli. P. 235, fig. 10: Photograph by Andrea Pozza.

"RESEARCH"
Pp. 240–41: Photograph by Infinite 3D (Charlie Coleman BIPP). P. 243: Photograph by Christian Glaeser. P. 244: Photograph by Pascal Lafay. P. 245: Photograph by Michael Strassen. P. 246: Camerphoto, Venezia. P. 247: Photograph by Lyndon Douglas. P. 264: Photograph by Infinite 3D (Charlie Coleman BIPP). Pp. 250–57: Photographs by David Adjaye.

MABEL O. WILSON, "OTHER MONUMENTALITIES"
P. 265, fig. 01: Smithsonian Institution Archives, image no. 18603. P. 266, fig. 02: Photograph © 2014 Allen Russ/Hoachlander Davis Photography, LLC. Pp. 280–81, fig. 11: Photograph by Edmund Sumner. P. 282, fig. 13: Photograph by Ed Reeve.